81

ALTERNATIVES TO THE PEACE CORPS

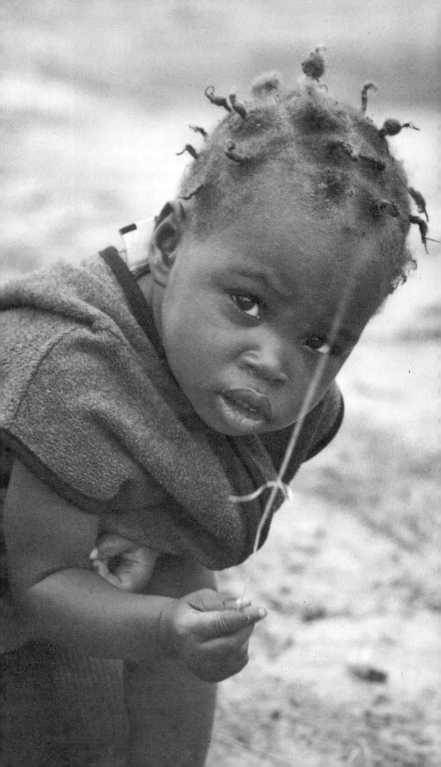

Alternatives to the Peace Corps

A Guide to Global Volunteer Opportunities

ELEVENTH EDITION

Edited by Paul Backhurst

FOOD FIRST BOOKS
OAKLAND, CALIFORNIA

Cover and interior design by Amy Evans McClure

Cover photograph: courtesy of WorldTeach (www.worldteach.org) and Annmarie Cholankeril, copyright Annmarie Cholankeril.

Photographs: pp. ii, 33 copyright Medair, Angola 2003; pp. 1, 36 courtesy of Global Vision International; p. 9 courtesy of El Porvenir; p. 31 courtesy of Global Exchange; p. 48 copyright Medair, Afganistan 2004; p. 85 copyright Medair

Eleventh edition, 2005

Food First Books
398 60th Street
Oakland, California 94618
www.foodfirst.org

CIP data on file with publisher
ISBN 0-935028-99-4

Food First Books are distributed by:
Client Distribution Services
425 Madison Avenue, Suite 1500
New York, NY 10017
(800) 343-4499

Printed in Canada

10 9 8 7 6 5 4 3 2 1

CONTENTS

PART II • Organizations and Resources

Acknowledgments

ALTERNATIVES TO THE PEACE CORPS has been developed in response to the numerous inquiries Food First receives from individuals seeking opportunities to gain community development experience.

Becky Buell, a staff member at Food First from 1985 to 1988, researched and wrote the original edition in 1986 with the assistance of Kari Hamerschlag, a Food First intern. Tremendous demand for the original book created a continuing need to revise and update it periodically.

Paul Backhurst updated and expanded the listings of volunteer opportunities for this eleventh edition, with help from Silvia Chiang and Clancy Drake.

This book is made possible by the organizations, volunteers, and friends who provide updates and additions each year. Many thanks go to the returned Peace Corps volunteers who have offered their perspectives in the development of this guide.

PREFACE

THE "WORLDWIDE WEB" IS AN APT DESCRIPTION OF MORE than just our Internet connections. Overall, the diverse peoples and nations of the world are becoming more and more mutually dependent. International volunteering is one of the more positive aspects of the globalization of our economies, cultures, and social and political structures. The more negative side of globalization emerges in trade pacts and common markets and through the consolidation of capital by a handful of multinational corporations, while the gap between rich and poor continues to increase. Volunteering is widely viewed as a way to support more broad-based development and promote social justice in troubled areas of the world, and the number, stature, and influence of volunteer-based organizations has increased markedly over recent decades. Under the auspices of numerous government agencies and nongovernmental organizations (NGOs), countless individuals have volunteered their time and resources to bring about social change.

The Cold War ushered in a special kind of international development aid that was part of a battle for the minds and loyalties of emerging nations. Established by President John F. Kennedy in 1961, the Peace Corps was intended to serve as a public relations tool to counter Soviet influence and, indeed, it was perceived as a form of benevolent foreign aid with a young American face. Tens of thousands of Americans have worked abroad through the Peace Corps since then, bringing home valuable experiences of foreign countries and the inner workings of government-sponsored aid. On the other hand, as we shall see in the next section, the Peace Corps has been strongly criticized for a number of reasons.

Since the Kennedy era, two generations of Americans have grown up supporting civil rights at home and seeking change in American foreign policy toward Vietnam, El Salvador, Nicaragua, South Africa, the Middle East, and a host of other regions. Many believe that US foreign policy has not always been helpful in building more equitable societies in developing nations. Neither human rights nor sustainable development has been the first priority of government foreign aid.

At Food First, we have researched world hunger extensively. Our analyses have led us to conclude that hunger is not caused by scarcity of food or poor people's lack of know-how or even overpopulation; it is caused by an unequal system of food production and distribution that enriches a small segment of society. Because of these inequalities, we emphasize the role of volunteers as participants in social change that is designed by and for local people.

Food First published the first edition of *Alternatives to the Peace Corps* in 1986 as a response to frequent requests for guidance on international volunteer opportunities that had no or minimal government strings attached. *Alternatives to the Peace Corps* was the first guide of its kind that offered options for voluntary service with private agencies that emphasized social change. The organizations and programs listed here seek volunteers who are willing to learn about local culture and support efforts by local grassroots organizations.

Another important priority in publishing *Alternatives to the Peace Corps* is to help place volunteers with agencies working for social and political reform in the United States. Hunger and poverty are not just foreign problems; here at home one in five children are growing up in poverty. The gap between rich and poor is increasing, creating a large underclass. Americans have always had a tradition of volunteer work; volunteerism has supported many of our community-based organizations, from parent-school groups and the YMCA/YWCA to coalitions against homelessness. Dedicated volunteers for self-help initiatives are needed more than ever today to counteract government cuts in programs for the disadvantaged, the elderly, immigrants, and the poor.

This eleventh edition of *Alternatives to the Peace Corps* is dedicated to the men and women, young and old, who want to share their talents with humanity to make this a better world.

Alternatives to the Peace Corps

PART I

Moving Beyond
the Peace Corps

Deciding to volunteer is difficult. Knowing why you want to volunteer is the first step toward choosing from among a huge variety of options: where to go, with what organization, and with what funds. A common solution to this dilemma is to choose a government-sponsored volunteer program, such as the Peace Corps of the United States, in which all expenses are paid, and training, health and accident insurance, travel expenses, and even a stipend are provided. Serving with a government agency may also seem inherently safer than traveling thousands of miles from home under the auspices of a tiny nongovernmental organization (NGO) working for social change. The Peace Corps name commands a level of recognition and respect that less well-known groups are hard-pressed to match.

This solution seems simple enough. But the Peace Corps and programs like it are not always as straightforward as they seem. The countries in which an agency works, the projects it supports, and the role of its volunteers have many political, social, and cultural implications. Volunteers are more than well-meaning individuals. They are representatives of the governmental, religious, or institutional values and objectives of the organization that sponsors them.

For example, the Peace Corps is an agency of the US government. The Peace Corps volunteer is part of the national team dispatched by the US State Department and is accountable to the US ambassador in the host country. The Peace Corps is inevitably linked to US foreign policy objectives, as is the Peace Corps volunteer.

The Peace Corps was founded by President John F. Kennedy to build America's positive image at home and overseas during the Cold War. In his 1961 inaugural address, Kennedy challenged young Americans to join "a grand and global alliance . . . to fight tyranny, poverty, disease, and war. . . ." The Peace Corps was ostensibly an apolitical organization, but its image was tainted from the outset by underlying foreign policy agendas. One initial goal of the Peace Corps was to counter Soviet cultural and political influence in developing nations; it was one tool used by the administration to eliminate the perceived threat of communism and to promote capitalism abroad.

The role of the Peace Corps in this agenda of the US government was no secret in its early years. A 1962 National Security Action Memorandum signed by Kennedy ordered the directors of the CIA, the United States Agency for International Development (USAID), and the Peace Corps to "give utmost attention and emphasis to programs designed to counter Communist indirect aggression [through] . . . support of local police forces for internal security and counterinsurgency purposes." Because the Peace Corps was closely linked to the CIA during its first decade, it lost credibility in some countries.

Prodded by a Senate committee investigating intelligence agencies in 1977, the CIA reported that it had not used the Peace Corps as a cover for its operations since 1975. The assertion may have been intended as reassurance, but it raises concerns about what those operations were and whether they continue today under a different dispensation. In 2003, the Russian government ended an 11-year contract with the Peace

Corps, accusing Peace Corps volunteers of attempting to gather information about Russian officials. Although these accusations were dismissed by the Peace Corps, they arise in the context of a history of questionable Peace Corps connections to the CIA and of touchy relations between the US and Russia. As we will explore further, the Peace Corps still has strong ties to the US government's foreign policy interests and is far from an apolitical organization.

The ideological underpinnings of the Peace Corps have altered to reflect the changing nature and objectives of US foreign policy over time. By the 1990s, US foreign policy was no longer defined primarily by the military influence of the Cold War but by its ability to mold societies through economic intervention. By influencing the patterns of resource control, legislation, and monetary policy within developing countries—whether through the International Monetary Fund (IMF) and World Bank's imposed structural adjustment programs or through free trade policies implemented by the World Trade Organization (WTO) and the North American Free Trade Agreement (NAFTA), the US government has found new ways to keep developing nations safe for its brand of capitalism.

The Peace Corps reflected this shift beginning in the 1980s. Under the leadership of director Loret Miller Ruppe during the Reagan administration, the Peace Corps began billing itself less as a symbol of goodwill and more seriously as a so-called development agency. Through initiatives such as the African Food System Initiative and the Competitive Enterprise Development Program, Peace Corps volunteers began promoting private enterprise and the development of export production in the rural sector.

The development of these programs coincided with economic policies handed down from the IMF and World Bank, which have pushed poor farmers away from growing basic food crops and toward planting specialty crops for foreign markets. This is economically risky and environmentally unsound and often results in farmers falling irretrievably into debt as they start planting for export and eventually lose their land. Many impoverished countries now import basic grains and legumes that were available locally and in great variety before. The net impact of these changes has eroded the standing of poor farmers and has contributed to the spread of hunger. Peace Corps volunteers in some countries abetted this agricultural shift despite their benevolent intentions.

This example of agricultural development points to a recurring theme in the history of the Peace Corps. While the stated goals of the Peace Corps and the intentions of Peace Corps volunteers are for the betterment of the world community, they are consistently undermined by US policies that perpetuate economic disparities and human rights abuses, as well as hinder development for poor communities. President Kennedy established the Peace Corps "to promote world peace and friendship." While Peace Corps volunteers are stationed across six continents, the US government leads the world in weapons sales and military training (to countries including Colombia, the Philippines, Pakistan, and Uzbekistan) and is one of the major advocates of IMF and World Bank structural adjustment programs. These policies promote neither peace or friendship with the people of developing nations, and as an instrument of US policy, the Peace Corps cannot escape being tainted by them.

Another example of well-intended Peace Corps projects coinciding with damaging US policies is the role volunteers often take as teachers. Peace Corps volunteers are assigned to teach a wide array of subjects in developing nations, from math to HIV/AIDS awareness. While these volunteers are devoting their time and energy to education, however, other US policies are harming the education systems in the very same countries. US–backed IMF and World Bank structural adjustment programs (required for nations to renegotiate their foreign debt) often require the governments of these nations to cut education budgets. US taxpayers pay about $80,000 for the training and service of each Peace Corps volunteer. That amount of money could pay the salaries of 40 or more local teachers in many of the countries where the Peace Corps runs programs.

The argument is often made that the Peace Corps simply goes where it is invited and does what it is asked to do. That's true, up to a point. But the projects the agency is willing to engage in and the numbers of volunteers it is willing to send— both with an eye to geopolitical interest—also enter into the equation. Foreign governments, not grassroots organizations, submit the requests for volunteers, and there is no guarantee that they have their citizens' best interests at heart.

US foreign policy and the US government's goals for the Peace Corps took a new turn following the events of September 11, 2001. In an effort to counter anti-American sentiment around the globe and particularly in the Middle East, President George W. Bush called for Americans to make a renewed commitment to volunteerism. In his 2002 State of the Union address, Bush unveiled the USA Freedom Corps, an umbrella organization to include the Peace Corps, AmeriCorps, and the Senior Corps, as well as a new Citizens Corps, whose purpose is to focus on the prevention of and emergency response to terrorism. President Bush called for the Peace Corps to double in size by 2007 and to expand its mission "to go into the Islamic world to spread the message of economic development and really share the compassion of a great nation." Thus the Peace Corps' mission has become repoliticized as part of the post-9/11 War on Terrorism: the Peace Corps is cited by the Bush administration as a tool in the fight to "overcome evil." In fact, Bush frequently blends his messages about terrorism with a call to public service. Although increased volunteerism is a noble request at a time when the world needs people working for positive change, the president's motives are made questionable by the fact that his calls for American service across the globe are accompanied by the dismantling and defunding of a myriad of social programs in the US and abroad, from sex education to affordable health care.

One Peace Corps volunteer's response to the new Freedom

Corps illuminates some of these contradictions. This volunteer, serving in the Ivory Coast, criticized Bush's proposal to double the size of the Peace Corps because "it wouldn't do much to alleviate the poverty and hopelessness that foster terrorism. For, in reality, the Peace Corps does more to make us Americans feel good about ourselves than it does to fight poverty. Instead, we need to change the economic policies that I often find are punishing the very villagers I am trying to help." He cited the farm subsidy bill signed by Bush in May 2002, which increased subsidies to US cotton growers while African cotton farmers have to sell their cotton in a market depressed partly by overproduction in the US. "Expanding the Peace Corps is a nice gesture. But if that's the sort of carrot we're using alongside the very big stick of US economic and military might, it isn't much of a meal. . . . What we really need to do is fill the stomachs and pocketbooks of the developing world."

If the Peace Corps is serious about its goal of capacity-building (in development lingo, imparting skills and knowledge rather than simply performing charity), then the Peace Corps may assist host nations right out of their need for the Peace Corps. This should not be considered a bad thing.

Volunteering for the Peace Corps

Many Peace Corps volunteers would argue that their placement had little or nothing to do with the larger policy objectives of the US government. One volunteer working in a mountain region of the Philippines had no contact with the Peace Corps office, USAID, or any other Peace Corps volunteer in his two years of service. "I arrived at the community and worked out my role with them," he explained. Most volunteers believe that their service had a positive impact, independent of the other agencies and policy initiatives of the US government. "I worked with women to develop composting techniques and planting vegetables," said a volunteer working in Honduras. "These are techniques that will benefit them for a lifetime."

Structural Adjustment

During the 1980s and 1990s international agencies such as the IMF and the World Bank forced structural changes on economies in the developing world. Loans desperately needed to restructure foreign debts were conditioned on the performance of "structural adjustment" programs—technocratic plans whose declared aim was to make economies more "efficient," "competitive," and capable of growth. In fact, a principal effect, and perhaps even aim, of these programs has been to pry open the economies of developing nations for foreign corporations, providing them with new markets and investment opportunities. This has been accomplished by imposing diverse free market policies, including privatization of state enterprises, deregulation (removal of restrictions on investment, both domestic and foreign), slashing of government budgets for health, education, and social services, and removal of import barriers. In country after country, the impact of these adjustments on the living conditions of the majority has been disastrous. Carried out on a large scale and in a very short time span, privatization transferred the benefits of institutions and resources from the general public to private businesses. In most countries, the gap between rich and poor widened as economic power became more sharply concentrated in increasingly fewer hands. As a result, poverty and hunger escalated in the developing world during the 1980s and early 1990s, especially in Latin America and Africa, where "adjustment" was more assiduously implemented by local elites. The IMF and World Bank continue to loan conditionally to developing nations. However, the IMF no longer refers to these as "structural adjustment" policies. In 1999, the IMF replaced the Enhanced Structural Adjustment Facility with the Poverty Reduction and Growth Facility, although the function is essentially the same.

(**Source:** *World Hunger: Twelve Myths,* by Frances Moore Lappé, Joseph Collins, and Peter Rosset, 1999, p. 103.)

Despite the fact that some Peace Corps volunteers have felt their work was autonomous from US government policy, the link is inherent, and federal lawmakers have referred to the connection as a matter of course. "If there is a person in the Peace Corps who feels he cannot support US foreign policy, then he ought not to be in the Peace Corps," stated Senator Ross Adair (R-Ind). Loret Miller Ruppe, director of the Peace Corps for eight years, proclaimed proudly at the outset of her tenure in 1981 that she hoped to prove her agency's work "a valuable source of real aid to US foreign policy."

In general, the Peace Corps discourages expressions of dissent from federal doctrine. During the Vietnam War, the Peace Corps stipulated that no public disapproval of the war would be tolerated, and in a widely publicized incident, a volunteer in Chile was dismissed after he wrote a letter denouncing the war to a Chilean newspaper. Yet even keeping one's views silent and working diligently to encourage real development may not be a sufficient shield from policy imperatives. A pair of volunteers in Honduras in the 1980s were commanded to "name the names" of local citizens that their sector boss believed were communists. Prospective volunteers should think carefully about how their political views may be inhibited by their placement with the Peace Corps.

Other criticisms have been leveled at the Peace Corps over the years. Former volunteers and staff have accused the agency of providing insufficient training, of defining goals and tasks too vaguely, and of withholding follow-through, thus hindering the long-term sustainability of projects. Returnees note that the Peace Corps often uses the presence or number of volunteers sent as a bargaining chip in its relations with other countries. During the 1980s, Central American nations allied with the US were flooded with volunteers to counterbalance the heightened US military presence there and to put a good face on the intervention against Sandinista Nicaragua.

Despite all the concerns about the Peace Corps as an arm of US foreign policy, the agency must be credited with enabling thousands of American citizens to witness the realities of poverty and injustice in developing nations. The refrain one hears over and over again in statements from returned volunteers is "I got much more than I gave." Most Peace Corps volunteers will attest that living and working alongside people in poor communities was the most powerful experience of their lives—one that has influenced their decisions and actions ever since. Many returned Peace Corps volunteers have learned through their placement about the intimate connections between development and economic justice, militarization and human rights. They return to the US and work to make US foreign and domestic policy more accountable to the poor.

As one returned Peace Corps volunteer explained, "If there is one thing to thank the Peace Corps for, it's for showing me how US policies hurt the average person. In a country like Paraguay, it is hard to miss the connection between US aid and the oppression of the poor. It is hard to miss the links between the IMF economic package and the inability of the poor to feed themselves. These realizations radically changed my perspectives on the world." But the Peace Corps is not the only way to have such valuable experiences.

United States Agency for International Development

A look at some of the other federal agencies involved in development work is in order. The US Agency for International Development (USAID), created by Kennedy in 1961, the same year as the Peace Corps, states frankly on its website that the purpose of US aid to other nations is to further America's foreign policy interests. Through field offices in foreign countries, USAID funnels monetary aid and technical assistance to projects that are in keeping with the purposes of foreign policy. Some of these projects have involved leaning on governments to privatize state-owned industries, allow greater foreign investment, and decrease spending on social programs such as health, education, and food subsidies. USAID has helped to uphold the regime of debt service imposed upon many poor countries by the IMF and the World Bank and to enforce the claims of US corporations conducting business abroad. Too often, the agency has pushed for costly solutions to local problems, and its projects have enriched only the wealthiest citizens of developing nations. In this guide, we have tried to avoid listing organizations that accept money from USAID.

VISTA and AmeriCorps

The government volunteer service program in the US, now known as AmeriCorps, offers another interesting comparison to the Peace Corps. In 1964, President Johnson created VISTA (Volunteers in Service to America) as the "domestic Peace Corps," and in 1993 under President Clinton, VISTA was replaced by the Corporation for National Service, or AmeriCorps. The purpose of both of these programs was and is to address issues such as homelessness, illiteracy, and economic and neighborhood revitalization through placements with nonprofits, public agencies, and faith-based organizations. As with the Peace Corps, volunteers are prohibited from engaging in political activity during their participation, and there can be little doubt that the stated aims of the projects AmeriCorps (and VISTA before it) supports seldom run counter to official US policy on poverty. Yet, in its early years, VISTA's emphasis on community organizing and self-help over service delivery—as well as its removal from the realm of foreign relations and the imperative of upholding our image overseas—garnered the agency a reputation for activism, even radicalism. VISTA later assisted with the implementation of and support for welfare reform legislation, which undermined its goal of reducing poverty. Over the years, VISTA gradually shifted its focus away from remedying poverty and toward more general service endeavors; it promoted volunteerism less as an agent of social change and more as a salutary and fulfilling activity for concerned citizens. Like USAID and the Peace Corps, its first concern is the proper placement and use of the aid giver, not the long-term needs of the aid receiver.

President Bush realigned AmeriCorps with domestic and foreign federal policies in 2002, when he asked for the expansion of AmeriCorps to assist with homeland security and the War on Terrorism. The Citizens Service Act that described this expansion also included changes to the pledge taken by AmeriCorps volunteers. Previously the pledge focused on community service, made no mention of the US Constitution, and had no religious references. In this bill, however, officials proposed a new pledge in which volunteers would promise to support the Constitution of the United States "in God's name." This pledge would be voluntary, but clearly there is a push in Washington for increased political and religious influence on AmeriCorps public service programs.

Nongovernmental Organizations

Much has been said and written over the last two decades about the proliferation of nongovernmental organizations throughout the world and their potential for enacting social and political change. In countries of the developing and developed world —of the global South and the global North—the last 20 years have witnessed a massive upsurge in the number of citizens' organizations airing grievances, lobbying for redress, mobilizing protests, establishing needed services for their constituents, and advocating for democratization of the forces of market and state. Concurrent has been the rise of resource or support organizations, often but not exclusively in the North, that provide research, advice, information, grants, or other aid to citizens' groups or to broader movements. In the North, both kinds of groups are generally referred to as NGOs, "civil society," or the "voluntary sector" or "third sector" (as in a sector separate from both the market and the state); in the US, NGOs are often called "nonprofits." Many in the global South distinguish between NGOs, which offer research and support, and civil society groups or social movements, which have a popular base. Lester Salamon, director of the Institute for Policy Studies at Johns Hopkins University, has used the term "associational revolution" to describe the growing size and strength of civil society groups of all kinds. Their appeal to believers throughout the political spectrum is considerable, and their successes have inspired much optimism that they can accomplish what market and state have failed to bring about. To name just one example, concerted networking among hundreds of civil society organizations put thousands of protesters on the streets of Seattle during the WTO's Third Ministerial Conference in 1999. This was the start of a growing global movement for economic and social justice, manifested in the streets of cities all over the world in the last few years.

However, the emphasis on third sector solutions can conceal a retreat from necessary government-supported solutions to poverty and injustice, such as agrarian reform or income redistribution. In the present day, when 51 of the hundred largest economies in the world are transnational corporations, one cannot be too complacent about the strength of the market or the role governments play in enforcing inequalities of wealth. The presence of the third sector in and of itself is not a cure for social problems. It is a powerful tool, but only one tool among several.

Nevertheless, the future of nongovernmental organizations and social movements appears promising. These days USAID and the Peace Corps employ the rhetoric of "grassroots empowerment" and "local decision-making" in describing their own projects. We welcome this sign of the trickling up of NGO influence and can only hope that there is sufficient substance behind the words to make a real difference in some people's lives.

The organizations in this book are, or work in cooperation with, NGOs and citizens' groups—not the government—in countries receiving volunteers. International cooperation among these groups is no guarantee against wasted or misguided efforts, but at least the work that gets accomplished is much less likely to be confused with or compromised by the agendas of government, either ours or someone else's. Readers of this book are encouraged to involve themselves in truly sustainable development. We can build international cooperation most effectively through the empowerment and leadership of local people.

2

Assessing Your Needs and Narrowing Your Search

CHOOSING A VOLUNTEER PROGRAM INVOLVES ASSESS-
ing your own ideals and personal needs and then finding
an organization or program that matches those best. You may
know that you want to work with children or on sustainable
development, or that you want to work with an organization
that is completely run by local people rather than one that is
based in the US or Europe. You may have only a month to volunteer or have financial constraints that affect the type of program you are able to do, or its location. In order to match your
needs it is important to be informed of the different possibilities and their strengths and weaknesses.

What Sorts of Projects Are Available?

In a few pages, we'll get to assessing your own needs and options
and evaluating organizations. First, though, let's take a look at
the types of opportunities that are available, and what their
benefits and drawbacks might be.

Long-Term Projects

The Peace Corps requires a two-year commitment from its volunteers, and this is not without good reason. Whether you are planning to volunteer in Zimbabwe or in Arizona, the more time you spend there, the better you will understand the community and the more you will be able to contribute. Particularly in the first months of your volunteer experience, you will mostly be learning from the people you are working with, and it takes a long time before you develop the knowledge and connections necessary to even begin to effect change. Drawbacks of this kind of commitment are obvious—a long-term, intensive experience is not for everyone. You may have other financial or time commitments, or family responsibilities, that keep you from taking on a volunteer stint of a year or more. And, if you are not going through an organization that offers a living stipend, you may worry about how you can support yourself as a volunteer for such a long time. If this is the case, read the section on fund-raising in this chapter—it has some suggestions for making a long-term volunteer commitment financially possible.

Short-Term Opportunities

While some organizations require a minimum six-month or one-year commitment from volunteers—and this is the best way to learn and contribute most effectively and deeply—you may not have the freedom to spend more than a month volunteering. Some of the organizations listed in the International and US sections of this book run shorter programs that focus on cultural exchange as well as service projects to benefit the community you are visiting. Be aware that a shorter term commitment will probably end up being more of a cultural exchange, and an excellent educational experience for you, than a chance to see a substantial service project through. However, a well-run program offering shorter term volunteer slots can still be of genuine service to a local community.

Alternative Travel

If your time is limited, you may also want to look into socially responsible trips and tours. Several organizations and travel agencies lead "reality tours" abroad. These are socially responsible educational tours that provide participants with firsthand experience of the political, economic, and social structures that create or promote hunger, poverty, and environmental degradation. Tours offer an opportunity to meet people with diverse perspectives on agriculture, development, and the environment. They often include the opportunity to stay with local people, visit rural areas, and meet with grassroots organizers. Such tours can alter your understanding of hunger and poverty and direct you to areas where you can best work for democratic social change. These are great opportunities for people who need a shorter term, intensive, and well-structured experience. However, these are not always the cheapest options and are usually more educational than service-oriented.

Volunteering as a Student

A number of universities offer study abroad programs that provide an opportunity to learn about the political, economic, and social conditions in a given country; several of these programs are listed in the Alternative Travel and Study Overseas section of this book. It is possible, however, to combine almost any sort of overseas study program with volunteer work, if you are enterprising. Once established in a country, seek out individuals and groups directly involved with community development. They may be able to direct you to an appropriate volunteer placement where you can build your skills and experience in the field. Working in this way can give you the contacts, experience, and confidence you may need for a longer or more intensive overseas experience when you are finished with school.

Professional/Skilled Exchange

Many organizations welcome volunteers with specific technical skills in such fields as construction, health care, and agriculture. If you have some years of experience in a particular area, working directly with an organization or community that needs people with your experience is a great opportunity for you. Organizations geared less toward accommodating American volunteers and more focused on local, grassroots work will often only accept volunteers with very specific skills that the organization is lacking and needs to further its work. This kind of volunteer opportunity is probably one of the best ways to do truly effective work for a community. The closer your skills match their needs, and the more involved you can be on a practical level, the more productive your experience will be for both you and the community you are working in. In any work experience, local people can best define your role. Let them know what your skills are and allow them to decide how they can best put those skills to use.

Working Overseas

Most overseas development positions require two or more years of community development experience. While a two-year volunteer post does not guarantee future employment, you may find that by developing your skills and connections with communities in the developing world, job possibilities will open up. To guide you in your job search, you will find organizations and publications in the Resources section that list employment openings overseas.

Designing Your Own Experience

For someone who has significant travel experience and a solid focus on the kind of work he or she would like to do abroad, this may be the best option. It can be a wonderful experience to design your own trip and project, especially if you have a unique schedule or already know the area you are traveling to. Just remember that the longer you stay in a community, the greater the difference you can make. Most of the organizations we have listed in this book are based in the US or Europe and make international connections for their volunteers. However, there are thousands of NGOs, both small and large, all over the world, and we could not possibly include all of them here.

You can begin by researching grassroots organizations and contacting them to find out more about their needs and the types of skills they can use. When designing your own experience, it is important to think carefully about the specific skills you can bring to an organization and to be up-front about what you can offer to the organizations you contact. A volunteer who went to work with a community organization in Mexico learned that his most useful skill was puppet making. He didn't know before he arrived that street theater is a popular form of political communication. When a local clinic learned that he was an artist and an actor, they suggested that he help them communicate health-care information through puppet shows.

In the Resources section of this book, we have included several publications and websites that list NGOs and other volunteer opportunities. The Internet is an invaluable resource for finding organizations. After spending an hour or two searching, you will probably have several organizations to contact, and you can begin to narrow your search depending on the needs and values of each organization. While researching and making connections from home is essential, it may be that you need to wait until you are in-country to figure out the details of your volunteer experience. Many small NGOs do not have Internet access, and you can only learn about them once you are there. The most important thing for you to do when you are working independently is to talk to people. The more people you meet and learn from, the more connections you will make and the more doors will open.

Keep in mind that it is a mistake to assume that all grassroots organizations need or want volunteers. Some groups are suspicious of the idea of unpaid labor in any context and prefer to retain only a tiny but paid staff. Some emphasize the values of mutual aid and local empowerment to the point of not wanting volunteers from outside the community served. Do not presume that, with a little coaxing or bargaining, you can overcome the resistance of someone who says no to your offer to volunteer. When you contact organizations, clearly state your goals, expectations, skills, and the length of time you are available. The organization can then decide if you can be of service in its work.

What Are Your Motivations?

Before committing to an organization, it is important to clarify your motives and your constraints. You may be drawn to voluntary service by a desire to help people striving for social, political, or economic change; you may be interested in learning about another culture and society; you may seek adventure; you may be eager to gain experience that will help you find a job. Your motivation may consist of all these reasons and more, to varying degrees. Thoroughly understanding why you want to volunteer can help you find a good organization, keep you focused and confident during your service, and ensure that you get the most from the experience.

Humanitarian motivations lead many prospective volunteers to communities plagued by extreme poverty and injustice. A volunteer may wish to feed the hungry, heal the sick, or house the homeless, but these social and political problems are often incredibly complex. Learning the dynamics of a community is the greatest challenge to a volunteer, making the volunteer's most appropriate role that of a student. An ill-advised motivation for volunteering can sometimes accompany the humanitarian impulse. This motivation might be called crusaderism —wanting to travel to far-flung pockets of deprivation and change everything in the space of three months. To expect too much from your volunteer experience is to set yourself up for disappointment. We might do well to heed the observation of Dorothy Day, cofounder of the Catholic Worker Movement in the 1930s, who assessed the slow pace of social change: "What we do is so little that we may seem to be constantly failing. . . . And why must we see the results of our giving? Our work is to sow—another generation will be reaping the harvest."

Concerned American citizens who want to help impoverished people don't need to travel around the globe to fulfill their goals. The challenges of community development here at home are immense. For this reason, one section of this book is dedicated to US organizations. Voluntary service in low-income communities in the US can also be a valuable educational experience or preparation for future work.

Another motivation for voluntary service is the desire to learn more about other societies. Living in another country can build your appreciation of the richness of other cultures and enable you to gain a comparative perspective on life in the United States. Shorter term experiences such as work brigades, study tours, and international education programs often offer a component of historical and theoretical insight into problems faced by the communities you visit. Many such programs are specifically designed for students. In this book, a number of tour, education, and shorter term programs are also listed in the Alternative Travel and Study Overseas section.

If your concern is to improve your qualifications for a career in development, an unconventional work experience may enhance your candidacy. The best programs place volunteers with local NGOs that have requested a volunteer for a specific purpose. In these circumstances, volunteers have a better chance of making a meaningful contribution. These placements often require some skills—computer, teaching, agriculture, appropriate technology, health care, or fund-raising. If you do not already have experience in these areas, it would be wise to develop specific technical skills that may be of use to an organization, as well as language competency.

Simple escapism—the desire to get away from home to evade personal problems or because you can't decide on a career—is an understandable impulse, but it's not the best motivation for volunteering. If you are troubled, preoccupied, or at loose ends, your effectiveness overseas will be diminished.

Evaluating an Organization

The listings in this book describe dozens of organizations that we think offer strong alternatives for overseas and domestic volunteer experiences. But the listings are just a start. In addition to this book, many resources are available for finding organizations on your own, such as the Internet, career counseling centers, your friends, and other books. A few ideas are listed in the Resources section at the back of this book. Take the time to explore the myriad of opportunities available, both in this book and beyond, to find the organization or project best suited to your needs, motivations, and skills. No matter which voluntary service organization you are considering, it is important to ask questions that allow you to evaluate its motives, methods, and effectiveness. You want to be sure that the organization you devote your time and energy to is in line with your goals and values before you commit to working with them. To help you in this process, here are some questions based on those we used to evaluate the organizations included in this book. You may think of others that will help you match an organization's values to your own.

- What is the political or religious affiliation of the organization? Is its purpose to convert or influence poor people to adopt new cultural, economic, or social values?

- What is the organization's mission statement? How does it actually work to accomplish its goals?

- Will you be taking a job that could be done by a local person? If you are offering a new skill to an area, does the program involve transferring that skill to local people? Are the organization's goals to make the program self-sustainable?

- Who funds the organization? Do the funding sources have political or religious affiliations that may influence the organization's programs?

- How does the organization choose its programs? Have local people requested help from volunteers? Or do staff, funders, or the organization's board determine its programs?

- Is the organization working with local or national governments?

- If the organization says it works with local groups or NGOs, find out what types of groups they mean and what type of partnership they have. For example, the organization might work with a local school on an environmental education project or with a women's group working for economic self-sufficiency.

- What sort of training and support can you expect as a volunteer?

To answer questions like these, look beyond the program's brochures. If possible, get a list of previous volunteers and ask them about their experiences: Did they get good training and support? Was the experience what they expected based on the organization's claims, and, if not, why not? You may also want to write to people in the field, finding out who is critical of the program and why. The section called Further Reading lists several books that take a critical look at development organizations overseas.

Whether you decide on an organized volunteer program, a tour, or decide to go on your own, it is essential to do your homework beforehand. Read as much as possible about the country (especially its history and politics), learn about groups working in the area, write in advance to groups that interest you, and talk to people at home who know about the area you are considering.

Fund-raising

One of the biggest challenges that comes with choosing an alternative to the Peace Corps is finding a way to finance your trip. While some agencies offer a stipend, insurance, or travel expenses, many smaller programs are not able to offer these benefits. Government or church organizations can often afford to be more generous, and this is a major reason people choose to work through these organizations. Making your desire to work at the grassroots level a reality will require a creative approach to fund-raising. Particularly if you choose to work with a small, local organization, it is highly unlikely that they will be able to help you with your expenses. Truthfully, they cannot afford to put their resources anywhere but directly into the community in which they are working.

The first thing you should do is come up with a tentative, itemized budget for your trip. Research the potential costs of each of your expenses before you begin fund-raising. Not only does this give you a goal to reach in your fund-raising efforts, it shows those you are asking that you have given thought to your budget and are asking for money you will actually need.

Below is a list of many of the items you should include:

- Transportation to and from the site (airline tickets are often the biggest expense for a trip to a nation where housing and food costs are minimal compared to the US)

- Program fee (consult the program you are interested in to find out what fee, if any, they require)

- Housing costs

- Food costs

- Transportation during your stay (buses, trains, etc.)

- Communication costs (stamps, phone cards, Internet fees)

- Spending money

- Medical insurance

- Visa fee

- Medicine

- Departure tax (from the airport abroad)

- Travel gear (this includes anything you may need to buy, such as mosquito nets, water filters, camping equipment, etc.)

- Passport application fee

- Other (e.g., student loan repayments or other obligations)

Airfare will be your primary expense; living in a developing nation, especially in rural areas, is by and large extremely affordable in comparison to living in the US. If you can arrange an internship or a work exchange (like teaching English) for room and board, your living expenses can be kept to a minimum. Ask the organization you'll be working with for suggestions about this, though it will probably be easier to arrange a work exchange once you are in-country. The best way to find out how much money you should expect to need for some of these items, such as transportation and spending money, is to ask people who have worked or lived in the area you are traveling to. Ask the organization you are going to work with, and volunteers who have worked with the organization in the past, about costs.

Once you have figured out an estimated budget, don't let the numbers daunt you! You can go about finding the funds to support your trip in several ways, and if you make a fund-raising plan and stick to it, you are very likely to raise the funds you need. Your plan should include efforts to raise funds from several sources (some of which are described below). Approaching several sources in a thoughtful manner will bring success more quickly than putting all your eggs in one basket and hoping for the best. Successful fund-raising requires equal parts research, creativity, perseverance, and willingness to ask for help.

Scholarships and Fellowships
These are often available through universities, and if you are enrolled in school, you should find out what resources are available for students wishing to travel to research or volunteer

abroad. Universities also offer stipends toward room and board expenses for internships or volunteer programs in the US. Public libraries, career service centers, and specialized libraries like the Foundation Center—which has branches throughout the country—are sources for information on grants and loans for anyone. You may also be able to find funding through your local government, private associations, or church groups. For example, the Rotary Club offers scholarships for foreign travel, and many churches support their parishioners in return for educational services upon return from an overseas trip.

Loans and Gifts

Friends and relatives are another possible source of funds. You may be able to arrange a personal loan, or ask your extended circle for small contributions using a well-written fund-raising letter that describes your project and what you'll use the money for.

Events and Exchanges

Consider organizing a fund-raising pancake breakfast, bake sale, or white elephant sale. Friends, family, club or church members, or local businesses may be willing to help you by donating time, space, food, services, or items for sale. One woman who traveled throughout Central America for a year started her own newsletter and asked friends and family to subscribe to help subsidize her living expenses. If you receive funding from individuals or organizations, your funders may appreciate a slide show or talk about your experiences upon your return—or, if you're inclined, start a weblog that will help them share your experiences as they happen.

Your Own Resources

One source of funds (maybe the main source) will be your own bank account. Part of your fund-raising plan will probably include working for a while to save money for a trip or using savings you already have. You may also consider selling some possessions to help finance your travels.

Bringing the Lessons to Life

Working with poor communities, whether at home or abroad, to confront the causes of hunger and poverty can have a long-lasting impact on your life. It can deepen your understanding of the tremendous power the US has over the lives of people around the world: to make and break governments; to affect the world economy through trade, investment, and foreign aid policies; and to influence economic priorities through USAID, the World Bank, the International Monetary Fund, and the World Trade Organization, among other entities.

The work will be educational, but that is only the beginning. Experience with a disenfranchised community means taking the responsibility of bringing your experiences home. The lessons you learn may have direct applications: working to end hunger and poverty in the US, pressuring the US government to end its involvement with repressive regimes, limiting arms sales to developing nations, and holding US corporations accountable for their actions, whether overseas or at home.

An experience in a developing nation can be translated into work at home in many ways. A Peace Corps volunteer who served with Guatemalan Indians returned to the US and worked with Native Americans in Arizona. A health-care volunteer with an international organization in Ghana found work at a free clinic in California. An agricultural extension worker who volunteered in Mozambique became active in the movement to stop US support of South Africa's apartheid regime. These examples and others show that experience in a marginalized community is often the catalyst for taking action in your own country to create more democratic organizations and politics at the local, national, and international levels, and to help ensure the survival of grassroots efforts all over the world.

3

How to Use This Book

IN COMPILING THE FOLLOWING LISTS OF ORGANIZATIONS, we looked for groups that address the political and economic causes of poverty. In our view, these programs place volunteers in positions that complement the work of local people, grass-roots organizations, and nongovernmental organizations (NGOs) by focusing on capacity building and providing services that are sustainable.

We made a few significant discriminations when deciding which organizations to include in this book. Organizations that rely on US government funding are not included because government money can never be completely free from Washington's agendas. A command of the English language has without question become a desirable attainment in many developing nations, but we list none of the organizations that deal strictly in sending English-speaking teachers overseas. We include only a few of the organizations devoted to sending teachers abroad, on the grounds that most of those programs serve primarily the host countries' middle or professional classes. We have tried to steer clear of any organizations that are evangelical, but we do list some volunteer programs with religious affiliations that hold as their primary purpose the support of local efforts at community development. Some do require a commitment to a certain faith, but most ask only that the volunteer share a concern for social justice. As with any volunteer placement, it is important to understand the values behind an agency's volunteer program clearly. We have done the initial screening, but you should investigate an organization thoroughly before you choose to work with them.

The listings are by no means comprehensive. Many organizations are so small and take so few volunteers that they prefer not to be listed, which is not to say that they would not like to be approached by informed and enterprising potential volunteers. Hundreds of other possibilities are not mentioned because they are so locally based that it makes more sense to find and contact them once you are abroad. We were only able to include a fraction of the organizations doing good work around the globe, so this book should be a launching point in your search for volunteer opportunities and commitment to social justice. Every community, school, church, and labor union has the potential for developing international programs that send delegates abroad, initiate ongoing partnership programs, and offer direct assistance to communities in developing nations or underserved communities in the US. These opportunities are often the most exciting, but must be created by the volunteer. (See the Designing Your Own Experience section in chapter 2 for more information.)

The organizations in this book are divided into four sections. The first two sections, International Voluntary Service Organizations and US Voluntary Service Organizations, are self-explanatory. In the Alternative Travel and Study Overseas section, you'll find organizations that sponsor short-term work projects, educational travel to frequently inaccessible areas of the world, and opportunities to study abroad. The last section, Resources, includes other organizations and guides, which do not sponsor regular volunteer programs but may distribute information or serve as a resource in your search.

We've added a few tools to this edition of *Alternatives to the Peace Corps* to aid you in using the book and searching for the best volunteer opportunity for you. There are two indexes at the back of the book, one alphabetical and one geographical. If you are looking for a volunteer program in a specific region of the world, refer to the geographical index. You will find icons beside the entries for many organizations included in this book to help you narrow your search quickly. The icons are meant to be a resource for you, but not a definitive word on any of these organizations. You should contact organizations directly with specific questions. A key for the icons appears below.

Key to Symbols

All of these organizations have a **religious affiliation**. Buddhism, Catholicism, and Judaism are just a few of the faith groups represented in this book. Some organizations are affiliated with a specific religious tradition, while others identify as interfaith. Most of these organizations do not require their volunteers be of a certain faith, and the emphasis on religion varies greatly among these groups.

These organizations request **proficiency in a foreign language** for participation in some or all of their programs. While some of these organizations require fluency in a foreign language, some say knowledge of a foreign language is helpful but not necessary.

These organizations offer some **short-term** volunteer opportunities of one month or less. (This icon does not appear in the Alternative Travel and Study Overseas section because most of the organizations listed in that section offer *only* short-term opportunities.)

These organizations all offer some kind of **financial assistance** to their volunteers. This ranges from groups that offer complete coverage of all expenses, including airfare, to organizations that provide modest monthly stipends abroad, to groups that offer a very limited number of scholarships.

Organizations
and Resources

PART II

4

INTERNATIONAL VOLUNTARY SERVICE ORGANIZATIONS

THE FOLLOWING ORGANIZATIONS OFFER OPPORTUNITIES to work abroad on a wide variety of issues and projects. These voluntary service organizations are selected for their common approach to combating injustices, emphasizing support of grassroots efforts around the globe. They are building international cooperation through the empowerment and leadership of local people.

Aang Serian "House of Peace"

PO Box 13732, Arusha, Tanzania or PO Box 19, Monduli, Tanzania
Tel: 011 (255 74) 431-8548
Fax: 011 (255 74) 574-4992
E-mail: aang_serian@hotmail.com or enolengila@yahoo.co.uk
Website: www.aangserian.org.uk
Contact: Mrs. Gemma B. Enolengila, International Liaison

Aang Serian is a nonreligious, nonsectarian NGO based in Tanzania whose principal mission is to develop cross-cultural curricula for rural schools. By emphasizing elements of indigenous culture that enhance self-respect, Aang Serian adapts traditional skills to empower people and help them eliminate poverty. Some experience living in a remote or challenging environment and some teaching background is preferred but not essential for potential volunteers over 18. Because curriculum development—in areas such as basic rural health care and sustainable agriculture—is an objective, placements of two months to one year at the Community School in Eluai are ideal for independent, experienced teachers interested in African cultures, who can handle "roughing it." Yet an Arusha town placement might work out for a disabled volunteer. For example, a placement with Nadumunye ("Arise") Women's Group, helping to develop markets for Fair Trade Maasai jewelry or to prepare grant applications, might work for someone with these interests and skills.

Volunteers should expect to pay a program fee of $350 plus their basic living costs and transportation, which should range $40–$50 per week. After consulting the website, interested persons may contact Aang Serian's international liaison.

Margaret S. Coventry, Volunteer, Aang Serian

I spent about a month with [Aang Serian] in Arusha, working together with the experienced main teacher at their new secondary school near Monduli. I had a good time with everyone connected with the project: I was warmly welcomed, respected but immediately involved with them, like a family.

The main work I did was to rewrite and expand the curriculum together with the teacher, and produce worksheets of reading passages and exercises in English but reflecting the culture of the rural Maasai herders and hunter-gatherers. The site of the school is difficult to access but I had one splendid day, visiting the school in the remote valley, meeting the local people, and celebrating the coming of the rains with them after a period of drought.

Adventures in Health, Education, and Agricultural Development, Inc. (AHEAD, Inc.)

PO Box 2049, Rockville, MD 20847-2049
Tel: (301) 530-3697
Fax: (301) 530-3532
E-mail: info@aheadinc.org
Website: www.aheadinc.org

AHEAD combats malnutrition, disease, and poverty through people-to-people exchanges and support of grassroots initiatives. Since 1985, AHEAD has provided unique opportunities for professionals as well as undergraduate and graduate students to work side by side with African counterparts in community projects there. Volunteers spend from one month to one year working in Tanzania or The Gambia with community development programs emphasizing teen pregnancy prevention, peer counseling, HIV/AIDS and STD prevention and treatment, immunizations, nutrition interventions, family planning, and vocational education.

The cost for the Summer Volunteer Program is $4,500. The fee covers round-trip international airfare; in-country travel, tips, taxes, and gratuities; accommodations and meals during work sessions; program costs; and one safari.

Volunteers are encouraged to raise funds for their trips or solicit sponsorships from family, church, school, community organizations, and local businesses. All contributions, including support for volunteers, are tax deductible.

Agencia Latinoamericana de Información (ALAI)

12 de octubre N18-24 y Patria, Of 503, Quito, Ecuador
Mailing address: Casilla 17-12-877, Quito, Ecuador
Tel: 011 (593 2) 250-5074 or 011 (593 2) 222-1570
Fax: 011 (593 2) 250-5073
E-mail: info@alainet.org
Website: www.alainet.org
Contact: Sally Burch, Executive Director

ALAI is a communications organization committed to human rights, gender equality, and people's participation in the development of Latin America. ALAI works for the democratization of communication. To that end, it has developed a model of alternative communication that aims toward the formation of a new fabric of communication that is democratic, widespread, decentralized, and multicultural.

ALAI accepts a few volunteers in its Quito office each year. Volunteers may assist with translation, journalism, or documentation work for ALAI's publications and website, or help design ALAI's website and databases. Volunteers are expected to cover their own expenses. ALAI welcomes applications from persons with disabilities, though no special facilities—other than elevator access to their office—exist.

Amazon-Africa Aid Organization (3AO)

PO Box 7776, Ann Arbor, MI 48107
Tel: (734) 769-5778
Fax: (734) 769-5779
E-mail: info@amazonafrica.org
Website: www.amazonafrica.org

3AO is an American nonprofit that partners with the Brazilian NGO Fundação Esperança to support the work of the Bill Chase Dental Clinic in the Brazilian Amazon. Located in the small city of Santarém, where the dark blue Tapajós waters flow into the muddy Amazon, the clinic provides necessary dental and other health-care services to an impoverished mixed-race community undergoing rapid social change. For over 30 years Fundação Esperança has been providing health care and education to the people of the Amazon. In an average year, the clinic's dental team perform over 26,000 procedures, including restorations, extractions, root canals, and X-rays. 3AO seeks accredited medical doctors and dentists who are willing to volunteer two to six weeks of their time at the dental clinic. The clinic will accommodate spouses, who often teach English to staff and students. Volunteers are asked to cover the price of their airfare to Santarém, but 3AO pays for room and board. Contact 3AO for more information.

American Friends Service Committee (AFSC)

International Programs' Volunteer Service
1501 Cherry Street, Philadelphia, PA 19102-1479
Fax: (215) 241-7247
Website: www.afsc.org

MEXICO SUMMER YOUTH PROGRAM
Tel: (215) 241-7295
E-mail: mexsummer@afsc.org

CHINA SUMMER WORK CAMP
Tel: (215) 241-7236
E-mail: arinh@pym.org (Arin Hanson) or ChinaWorkcamp@pym.org
    (Adam Clark-Valle)

AFSC, a Quaker organization founded in 1917 to promote justice and peace, has two volunteer opportunities: Mexico Summer Youth Program and China Summer Work camp.

Sowing Futures (*Semilleros de Futuros*), a summer project in Mexico, offers an opportunity for persons 18 to 26 from various countries and local indigenous communities to work together—to address political, social, ecological, and economic challenges while sharing their diverse cultures and experiences. Participants must be able to converse in Spanish; have interest in regional political, social, and cultural issues; and demonstrate the ability to work collectively and take on new challenges. Participants should be prepared to live in remote areas, under rural living conditions. The program runs for approximately seven weeks beginning at the end of June. A project fee of $1,250 is required, which includes food, lodging, and project materials, but travel expenses are not included. Scholarships are available for people with demonstrated financial need. The project is run in collaboration with Servicio, Desarrollo, y Paz, A.C. (SEDEPAC), a prominent Mexican NGO.

The work camp in Xiaoshicun, Hunan Province, which

brings together participants from the US, Japan, South Korea, and China, runs from late July to the third week of August. Volunteers teach English and computer skills to 150 local middle-school students and work together on joint environmental projects. Other than an overnight stay with a Chinese family, participants live in a century-old schoolhouse in same-sex (seven- to eight-person) dormitories. The US participant fee of $2,200 covers all expenses (including airfare) except personal incidentals. This project is jointly sponsored by AFSC and the Philadelphia Yearly Meeting.

Amigos de las Américas (Amigos) $ 88 ▧

5618 Star Lane, Houston, TX 77057
Tel: (800) 231-7796
Fax: (713) 782-9267
E-mail: info@amigoslink.org
Website: www.amigoslink.org

Amigos accepts volunteers 16 years and older who have studied the equivalent of two years' high school Spanish or Portuguese. Since 1965 Amigos has prepared enthusiastic, culturally sensitive volunteers to live with host families and work alongside community members helping provide public health services, community development, or children's education. Project placements last from four to eight weeks between June and August and occur in one of eight countries: Brazil, Costa Rica, Dominican Republic, Honduras, Mexico, Nicaragua, Panama, and Paraguay. Volunteers work in teams of two to three. Former Amigos projects have included: community-based initiatives, latrine and stove construction, environmental education, nutrition workshops, community garden organizing, health education, school renovations, rabies vaccinations, and youth group and sports league formation.

Amigos chapters across the US conduct training prior to departure and raise funds for the majority of the volunteers. College students and individuals who do not live in cities with chapters can apply as correspondent volunteers through the headquarters in Houston. Your cost, which includes international airfare from Houston or Miami, housing with a family, food, project supplies, transportation, and short-term medical insurance, ranges from approximately $3,475 to $3,700. We strongly encourage participant fund-raising, but need-based financial assistance is available. Current project information can be found on the website.

Amizade, Ltd.

PO Box 110107, Pittsburgh, PA 15232
Tel: (888) 973-4443 or (412) 441-6655
Fax: (412) 648-1492
E-mail: volunteer@amizade.org
Website: www.amizade.org

Amizade encourages intercultural exploration and understanding through community-driven service-learning courses and volunteer programs. In communities on five continents, over 1,000 Amizade volunteers have cooperated with community members to complete sustainable, community-identified projects that address needs in education, the environment, health, and well-being. Within the context of a unique cross-cultural experience that offers educational and recreational opportunities, Amizade volunteers have constructed an orphanage that houses 40 children in Bolivia, built a vocational training center for street children in the Brazilian Amazon, and completed historical restoration and environmental preservation in the Greater Yellowstone Area. Volunteers do not need any special skills, just a willingness to help. Current opportunities exist in Australia, Bolivia, Brazil, Nepal, the US, and several other countries around the world.

Amizade offers prescheduled programs for individuals and customized programs for groups. Additionally, through a partnership with the University of Pittsburgh, the Amizade Global Service-Learning Center facilitates courses that combine intercultural service and academic coursework for college credit. Volunteer program fees, which include room and board; transportation during the program; recreational, cultural, and educational activities; Amizade staff and administration fees; and a donation to the community, range from $475 to $1,895.

(Also listed under Alternative Travel and Study Overseas)

Bikes Not Bombs
(See listing under US Voluntary Service Organizations)

Brethren Volunteer Service (BVS) $ 🏚
1451 Dundee Avenue, Elgin, IL 60120
Tel: (847) 742-5100 or (800) 323-8039
Fax: (847) 742-0278
E-mail: bvs_gb@brethren.org
Website: www.brethrenvolunteerservice.org

BVS is a program grounded in the Christian faith that brings a spiritual dimension to advocating justice, working for peace, serving basic human needs, and maintaining the integrity of creation. BVS places volunteers in Latin America (Dominican Republic, Guatemala, Honduras, Nicaragua), Europe (Belgium, Bosnia-Herzegovina, Czech Republic, France, Germany, Ireland, Netherlands, Poland, Serbia-Yugoslavia, Slovakia, UK-Northern Ireland), Asia (Japan), and Africa (Nigeria). BVS also has one-year programs in the US. Positions abroad last two years and begin with a three-week orientation in the US. Volunteers are involved in a variety of community services: education, health care, office/secretarial work, and construction work. Volunteers can also participate in ministry to children, youth, senior citizens, homeless, victims of domestic violence, prisoners, refugees, and persons with AIDS. Some positions require knowledge of a foreign language prior to orientation. Other requirements and special skills vary with assignments. Volunteers need not be Brethren or Christian but should be willing to examine the Christian faith. A college degree or equivalent life experience is required for overseas assignments. Travel expenses, room and board, medical coverage, and a monthly stipend of about $60 are provided. Some persons with physical disabilities can be accommodated, depending on the project.

Centro de Investigaciones Económicas y Políticas de Acción Comunitaria, A.C. (CIEPAC)

Calle de la Primavera, No. 6, Barrio de la Merced C.P. 29240,
San Cristóbal de las Casas, Chiapas, Mexico
Tel/Fax: 011 (52) 967-674-5168
E-mail: ciepac@laneta.apc.org
Website: www.ciepac.org
Contact: Miguel Pickard

CIEPAC is an alternative to mainstream sources of information in Mexico, empowering citizens and citizen organizations to use information to create their own analysis, spaces for participation, and alternatives. Projects include weekly analysis bulletins, grassroots analysis forums with indigenous communities, education of the "first world," and elaboration of popular education materials, all to strengthen local, national, and international movements for justice.

CIEPAC usually accepts volunteers to work for a minimum of two months, and for a maximum of six months. Volunteers help research topics of interest to the Center through the Internet or by other means, and may help to write about the effects of globalization on the communities in Chiapas, depending on their experience and expertise. Volunteers should be proficient in Spanish and are expected to pay all costs. For further information in English and Spanish, refer first to the CIEPAC website and then to the "Cooperantes" button on the left side.

Child Family Health International (CFHI)

953 Mission Street, Suite 220, San Francisco, CA 94103
Tel: (415) 957-9000
Fax: (415) 840-0486
E-mail: info@cfhi.org
Website: www.cfhi.org

CFHI is a nonprofit organization providing health services to underserved communities worldwide by supporting local projects with essential medical supplies, volunteers, and funding. CFHI sends US medical, premedical, nursing, and other public health students to Bolivia, Ecuador, India, Mexico, and South

Africa for training and service learning. Duties include hospital or clinical rotations and community education and outreach.

Participants should view their experience as an opportunity to develop cross-cultural and community health awareness, rather than to provide humanitarian aid. Programs vary in length from four to eight weeks. Spanish language proficiency is useful for many of the placements, though language courses often are included in the program. Fees vary by program. Scholarships are available on a limited basis. Alumni services, including grants for health-care projects, are available. Refer to the website for more details.

Christian Peacemaker Teams (CPT)

PO Box 6508, Chicago, IL 60680-6508
Tel: (773) 277-0253
Fax: (773) 277-0291
E-mail: peacemakers@cpt.org
Website: www.cpt.org

CPT places teams of international volunteers in conflict settings as a violence-reduction presence. CPT is cross-denominational with strong roots grounded in the Quakers, Mennonites, and Church of the Brethren. CPT organizes long-term volunteers—the Christian Peacemaker Corps—to perform protective witness and accompaniment work in Colombia, Iraq, Palestine, and with Native Canadian communities in Ontario. Teams of 4 to 12 persons join the efforts of local peacemakers facing imminent violence. They accompany threatened individuals, report on human rights abuses, plan and execute nonviolent public responses to injustice, and train others in nonviolent direct action.

CPT emphasizes the Christian nature of its commitment to peace. All Christian Peacemaker Corps volunteers must attend training in nonviolent direct action, conflict de-escalation, and team building, either at CPT headquarters in Chicago or at regional sessions. Candidates pay their own way to training; if accepted, full-time corps members receive a small monthly stipend based on their living expenses and are expected to seek contributions to CPT in support of their work. CPT also maintains a Reserve Corps of trained volunteers who are on call for short periods of time. Corps volunteers and reservists must be 21 or older.

(Also listed under Alternative Travel and Study Overseas)

Christians for Peace in El Salvador (CRISPAZ)

122 DeWitt Drive, Boston, MA 02120
Tel: (617) 445-5115
Fax: (617) 249-0769
E-mail: info@crispaz.org
Website: www.crispaz.org

Founded in 1984, CRISPAZ is a faith-based organization dedicated to working with poor and marginalized communities in El Salvador. In building bridges of solidarity between communities in El Salvador and those in their home countries, CRISPAZ volunteers strive together for peace, justice, and human liberation. The long-term volunteer program is designed for individuals who wish to spend a minimum of one year living and working in a marginalized urban or rural community in El Salvador (with cultural immersion and orientation allow 15 months). Long-term volunteers give of their time, skills, and interests as they work alongside Salvadorans in areas such as literacy, health care, pastoral work, community organization, education, agriculture, appropriate technology, and youth work.

The summer immersion program is designed to provide an intensive learning and service experience in a poor community in El Salvador. Interns live with Salvadorans and accompany them in their daily lives and work. Each intern will have the opportunity to contribute his or her skills to the communities. CRISPAZ provides volunteers with orientation, project placement, and support throughout the term of service.

(Also listed under Alternative Travel and Study Overseas)

Concern America

2015 North Broadway, Santa Ana, CA 92706
Mailing address: PO Box 1790, Santa Ana, CA 92702
Tel: (714) 953-8575 or (800) 266-2376
Fax: (714) 953-1242
E-mail: concamerinc@earthlink.net
Website: www.concernamerica.org

Concern America is an international development and refugee aid organization whose main objective is to provide training, technical assistance, and material support to community-based programs in developing countries and refugee camps. Concern America volunteers serve for at least two years and are professionals such as physicians, nurses, nutritionists, community organizers, and specialists in agriculture, appropriate technology, public health, and sanitation. The focus of the work is on training local people to carry on programs that include health-care training, developing nutrition and sanitation projects, organizing community development and income-generating projects, and conducting literacy campaigns. Concern America volunteers currently serve in Colombia, El Salvador, Honduras, Guatemala, Guinea, Mexico, and Mozambique. Volunteers must be at least 21 and fluent in Spanish (if serving in Latin America). Concern America provides transportation, room and board, health insurance, a small stipend, and a repatriation allowance.

Cross-Cultural Solutions (CCS)

2 Clinton Place, New Rochelle, NY 10801
Tel: (800) 380-4777 or (914) 632-0022
Fax: (914) 632-8494
E-mail: info@crossculturalsolutions.org
Website: www.crossculturalsolutions.org

CCS' international volunteer programs let you see the world—and yourself—from a whole new perspective. Programs are available in Brazil, China, Costa Rica, Ghana, Guatemala, India,

Peru, Russia, Thailand, and Tanzania. CCS believes that people know what is appropriate for their own communities. By participating in a CCS program, volunteers have the opportunity to work side by side with local people on sustainable community initiatives, which are locally designed and driven. This type of interaction leads to the sharing of perspectives and the fostering of cultural understanding—both essential parts of the CCS mission.

CCS volunteers are placed individually, based on an assessment of their unique skills and interests, with locally based partner programs. They work with infants and children, teenagers, adults, the elderly, and people with special needs like HIV/AIDS patients or the mentally or physically disabled. CCS has discovered that when volunteers are given the opportunity to learn about local culture and customs and understand community development, their experience is truly complete. To help the volunteers gain this inside perspective, all the programs offer cultural and learning activities, including a detailed orientation, language training, field trips, guest speakers, and participation in local activities. Volunteers have free time most evenings and every weekend to reflect on their experience and become more familiar with the local people and culture.

CCS has a home-base structure in each country, which provides safe and comfortable accommodations in a local community. The staff is from the local community, and your daily needs, such as meals and transportation, are all taken care of. Volunteers decide when, where, and how long they want to take part in a program. CCS' international volunteer programs range from 2 to 12 weeks (longer programs can be arranged). The program fee starts at $2,279 and is tax deductible in the US.

Helen Barr, Volunteer, Cross–Cultural Solutions

As a result of [CCS'] care in matching volunteer skills, interests, and hopes to programs, my volunteer time in Thailand and Peru exceeded expectations. I spent no longer than six weeks in each place but I felt the time I spent with street children in Bangkok and in Lima mattered in their day-to-day experiences. Alongside such disadvantage, learning about its causes and helping to make daily life for those children creative, fun, and, most of all, safe, I felt my presence did matter. Days matter.

It's now nearly a year since my first program in Thailand. Not a day goes by when I do not think of the people I worked with. The work does not stop once you come home; volunteering does not stop once the TV screen hoves into view again—by stepping into the space behind, you've crossed that all-important barrier.

Doctors for Global Health (DGH)

PO Box 1761, Decatur, GA 30031
Tel/Fax: (404) 377-3566
E-mail: volunteer@dghonline.org
Website: www.dghonline.org

DGH is a private nonprofit organization promoting health and human rights with those who have no voice. Founded in 1995, DGH strives to promote health, education, social justice, and human rights by funding and carrying out projects in coopera- tion with local nonprofit and nongovernmental partner organ- izations in interested communities. With an emphasis on community-oriented primary care, liberation medicine, and volunteerism, DGH accompanies communities in El Salvador, Nicaragua, Mexico, Guatemala, Uganda, and the United States. Various volunteer opportunities are available, depending on the volunteer's skills and the needs and desires of the local community. Most volunteer activities involve health-care, education, and public health activities. DGH prefers long-term volunteers but does occasionally accept volunteers for minimum stays of one to two months. Volunteers should expect to pay for their own travel expenses, food, and lodging.

Doctors Without Borders USA, Inc.
Médecins Sans Frontières USA, Inc. (MSF)

IN NEW YORK:
333 7th Avenue, 2nd Floor, New York, NY 10001-5004
Tel: (212) 679-6800 or (888) 392-0392
Fax: (212) 679-7016
E-mail: doctors@newyork.msf.org
Website: www.doctorswithoutborders.org

IN LOS ANGELES:
2525 Main Street, Suite 110, Santa Monica, CA 90405
Tel: (310) 399-0049
Fax: (310) 399-8177
E-mail: msf-losangeles@msf.org

Doctors Without Borders (known internationally as Médecins Sans Frontières, or MSF) is the world's largest independent emergency medical relief organization. Each year over 2,500 doctors, nurses, other medical professionals, and logistical experts from 45 nations volunteer to work in nearly 80 countries around the world. They assist victims of war, civil strife, epidemics, and natural disasters without discriminating between races, religions, creeds, or political affiliations.

Solid professional experience is essential in the field. All medical professionals must have a valid license to practice and have had two years of post-graduate professional work experience. The minimum volunteer commitment is six months; a year's commitment is more typical. A good working knowledge of a foreign language is highly valued. Familiarity with tropical medicine is an asset. For more information or an application form, please call or visit the website.

ESPWA, Inc.

PO Box 2071, Roseau, Commonwealth of Dominica
Tel: (767) 449-0322
E-mail: espwa@espwa.org
Website: www.espwa.org

Named for the Creole word meaning "hope," ESPWA has welcomed volunteers since 1996 to assist the endeavors of organizations working for sustainable communities. The focus now is entirely on organic agriculture and assistance to small organic farmers. Volunteers are usually headquartered in the Commonwealth of Dominica (not to be confused with the Dominican Republic). While types of work vary, they are primarily physical: construction, painting, composting, mapping and surveying, preparing fields for farming, and trail maintenance. Volunteers with special skills may be assigned such tasks as creating websites, researching and documenting environmental conditions, and planning educational materials.

Projects that ordinarily last from one to three weeks are for independent volunteers, students, and families. Longer term placements are available to project alumni. Volunteers pay their own expenses: transportation, incidental expenses, and a registration fee. These are tax deductible to the extent allowed by law. Accommodations at most project sites are simple, consisting of tents, a dormitory, or the village schoolhouse. English is the working language. Technical skills are not required, but a curious, adaptable, and adventurous mind is indispensable. They endeavor to accommodate people with physical disabilities.

Fellowship of Reconciliation (FOR)
Colombia Peace Presence

Task Force on Latin America and the Caribbean
2017 Mission Street, Suite 305, San Francisco, CA 94110
Tel: (415) 495-6334
Fax: (415) 495-5628
E-mail: forcolombia@igc.org
Website: www.forusa.org/programs/Colombia

The FOR Colombia Peace Presence offers protective accompaniment to the northern Colombian Peace Community of San José de Apartadó, which has taken an extraordinary nonviolent stand against war, refusing to support any armed participants in Colombia's decades-long war. The community has suffered terribly from political violence, mostly by paramilitary groups supported by the Colombian Army. Besides providing protective accompaniment, volunteers learn and report about other civil-society efforts to build peace (such as other peace communities, networks, and grassroots alternatives to war). Volunteers are placed either in San José de Apartadó or in the capital, Bogotá. To ensure the continuity of the Colombia Peace Presence, FOR seeks committed and skilled volunteers ready to accompany people striving for a life in peace and dignity. FOR is an interfaith organization.

Focus on the Global South
(See listing under Resources)

Foundation for Sustainable Development (FSD)
870 Market Street, Suite 321, San Francisco, CA 94102
Tel/Fax: (415) 283-4873
E-mail: info@fsdinternational.org
Website: www.fsdinternational.org

FSD is a private nonprofit organization dedicated to supporting sustainable development initiatives in Latin America, Africa, and Asia. Programs include an internship with a nonprofit development organization, family home stay, orientation, debriefing, and in some cases language training and group trips. Programs stress complete immersion and place only one intern in each organization and family. While internship programs are available throughout the year, for two months to one year, the summer programs have set dates and last between eight and ten weeks. Internships are available in a variety of areas and include education, community development, human rights, environment/conservation, microfinance, women's issues, health, nutrition, youth development, and many more. Programs are located in Argentina, Bolivia, Ecuador, India, Kenya, Nicaragua, Peru, Tanzania, and Uganda. Interns compete for small grants to fund in-country development projects. Short-term volunteering, study tours, and alternative spring breaks are also available. For more information about the application process and for internship descriptions, please see the website. Program costs vary. Credit and scholarships may be available.

Kate Vyborny, Volunteer, Foundation for Sustainable Development

At 11 pm the meeting is not even close to over. Two men and a woman in traditional Salasca dress shout at the same time, arguing in Quechua about how the profits from a cheese-making project will be divided. Several women in the meeting breastfeed their babies as they listen; children play outside, some getting tired and deciding to walk home alone through the dark fields. The president of the community occasionally breaks in and translates into Spanish for me....

A group of traditional artisans asked for help exporting their weavings, and I looked for Fair Trade suppliers; then I helped them apply to sell their work to these organizations. I had the privilege of serving two indigenous communities in rural Ecuador, and experiencing the challenges of community development firsthand. It was part of my job to attend meetings like this, hear what the people here hope for to improve their lives, and try to help make it happen.

Fourth World Movement/USA

7600 Willow Hill Drive, Landover, MD 20785-4658
Tel: (301) 336-9489
Fax: (301) 336-0092
E-mail: nationalcenter@4thworldmovement.org
Website: www.4thworldmovement.org

Fourth World Movement's work is based on three priorities: learning from the most disadvantaged families, understanding how they become trapped in persistent poverty, and planning and developing projects with them. Volunteers must first participate in a two- to three- month internship, living and working with full-time volunteers at the New York, New Orleans, or Washington DC area centers. Interns learn about Fourth World Movement and its approach to persistent poverty through their work, and through videos, readings, and discussion. At the end of the internship, volunteers discuss with their supervisor what their two-year assignment will be. Placement is made according to both an intern's interests and Fourth World's needs. There are currently teams in 26 countries and six continents. Participants contribute toward food costs during the internship and receive a small stipend during their assignment.

(Also listed under Alternative Travel and Study Overseas)

Frontier Internship in Mission (FIM)

International Coordinating Office
Ecumenical Center
150 Route de Ferney, 1211 Geneva 2, Switzerland
Tel: 011 (41 22) 798-8987
Fax: 011 (41 22) 788-1434
E-mail: jm@tfim.org
Website: www.tfim.org

FIM is an international ecumenical internship program that provides people between 20 and 35 years of age with the opportunity to work abroad on social issues for two years. The program emphasizes new forms of ecumenical mission in the context of justice, peace, and the ecosphere. FIM supports community building, especially among poor people's organizations in Asia, Africa, and Latin America. Individuals applying to FIM should be members of a community engaged in justice concerns. Communities interested in receiving an intern propose a project to FIM; communities wanting to send an intern to another region may also apply. The FIM coordinating office funds travel expenses, provides a subsistence living allowance, and coordinates a one-year reentry project with the intern's sending group after the two-year period overseas.

Frontiers Foundation/Operation Beaver
419 Coxwell Avenue, Toronto, Ontario M4L-3B9, Canada
Tel: (416) 690-3930
Fax: (416) 690-3934
E-mail: frontiersfoundation@on.aibn.com
Website: www.frontiersfoundation.ca

Frontiers Foundation is a community development service organization that works in partnership with communities in low-income rural areas across northern Canada. These locally initiated projects build and improve housing, conduct training programs, and organize educational and recreational activities in developing regions. Volunteers must be 18 or older and available for a minimum of 12 weeks. Skills in carpentry, electrical work, and plumbing are preferred for construction projects. Previous social service and experience with children are preferred for recreation and education projects. Accommodations, food, and travel inside Canada are provided.

Global Routes
1 Short Street, Northampton, MA 01060
Tel: (413) 585-8895
Fax: (413) 585-8810
E-mail: mail@globalroutes.org
Website: www.globalroutes.org

Global Routes, a tax-exempt nonprofit, is a nongovernmental, nonsectarian organization that designs experiential community service projects and teaching internships for high school and college-aged students. By living and working with people in rural communities throughout the world, program participants gain a better sense of themselves, the world, and their place in it.

High school programs are three, four, and five weeks long in the summer. Destinations include Belize, China, Costa Rica, Ecuador, the Dominican Republic, Ghana, Guadeloupe, India, Mexico, New Zealand, Puerto Rico, St. Lucia, and Thailand. The college-level teaching internship is 7 to 12 weeks long and offered in the summer, fall, winter, and spring. Programs currently exist in Costa Rica, Ecuador, Ghana, St. Lucia, and Thailand. All Global Routes programs have trained staff members onsite. Participants pay program fees and airfare.

Global Vision International (GVI)
Amwell Farm House, Nomansland, Wheathampstead,
   St. Albans, AL4 8EJ, United Kingdom
Tel: 011 (44 870) 608-8898
Fax: 011 (44 158) 283-4002
E-mail: info@gvi.co.uk
Website: www.gvi.co.uk
Contact: Chris Ash

GVI is a large UK-based NGO that works closely with much smaller partner organizations in many countries to meet their needs for caring, committed volunteers, material support, and promoting awareness of their projects. The focus is on sustainable, locally initiated development projects, ecological conservation, and cross-cultural education. Volunteers between the ages of 18 and 65 without prior experience commit to a term from two weeks to two years (the average being three months). With projects like monitoring sea turtles in Panama, GVI offers a wide range of interesting programs that will particularly appeal to college students wanting to take a summer or semester doing something worthwhile. The current volunteer cost for the program is $1,285, which includes comprehensive training.

Consult the website for current programs in these countries: Bolivia, Brazil, Chile, Costa Rica, Ecuador, Egypt, Guatemala, Honduras, Mexico, Namibia, Nepal, Panama, Peru, Rwanda, Seychelles, South Africa, Spain, and Sri Lanka.

Global Volunteer Network (GVN)

PO Box 2231, Wellington, New Zealand
Tel: 011 (64 4) 569-9080
Fax: 011 (64 4) 569-9081
E-mail: info@volunteer.org.nz
Website: www.volunteer.org.nz
Contact: Colin Salisbury, Executive Director

GVN supports local community organizations in developing countries through the placement of international volunteers. Opportunities are currently available in Alaska (US), China, Ecuador, El Salvador, Ghana, Nepal, New Zealand, Romania, Russia, Thailand, Uganda, and Vietnam. Volunteers can be involved in areas such as teaching English, environmental work, animal welfare, and health education. Program placements range from two weeks to a year, and are available to those aged 18 and up. While relevant experience enables volunteers to further enhance our programs, most do not require specialist skills. People with physical disabilities considered on a case-by-case basis. The application fee is $297, followed by monthly program fees ranging from $250 to $700, which cover the volunteer's food, housing, and most other in-country expenses.

Global Volunteers (GV)

375 East Little Canada Road, St. Paul, MN 55117-1627
Tel: (800) 487-1074 or (651) 407-6100
Fax: (651) 482-0915
E-mail: email@globalvolunteers.org
Website: www.globalvolunteers.org

GV, which was founded in 1984, forms teams of volunteers who live in host communities and work with local people on development projects selected by local leadership. The projects may involve construction and renovation of schools and clinics, health care, child care, tutoring, business planning, or assisting in other local activities. Opportunities are available in Africa, Asia, Australia and the Pacific Islands, Europe, Latin America and the Caribbean, and the US. Volunteers are of all ages and come from all backgrounds and occupations, including teachers, carpenters, homemakers, physicians, and artists. No special skills or languages are required. Tax-deductible program fees range from $750 to $2,695 and include costs of training, ground transportation, lodging, project materials, all meals, and an experienced team leader. Besides its service programs, the organization offers child-sponsorship programs in China, India, and Romania. GV has been designated a nongovernmental organization in special consultative status with the UN Economic and Social Council.

Hands for Help Nepal

Nawasangam Marg 10, Samakhusi, PO Box 9012,
    Kathmandu, Nepal
Tel: 011 (977 1) 4362648
Fax: 011 (977 1) 4477018
E-mail: hforh@ntc.net.np
Website: www.handsforhelp.org.np

Hands for Help Nepal is a nonprofit, nongovernmental organization that works throughout Nepal to provide English teaching and training, to raise awareness about environmental, health-care, and gender issues, and to provide training toward economic self-reliance for Nepali people. Programs last from one to five months in Nepal (five months is the tourist visa limit). Volunteers must be at least 17 years old. The cost is $500 for the first month and $100 for each additional month. Contact the program director, Anil Bhusal, at the above address for further information.

Housing and Land Rights Network
(HLRN)–South Asian Regional Program (SARP)
Habitat International Coalition (HIC)

B-28 Nizamuddin East, New Delhi 110013, India
Tel/Fax: 011 (91 11) 2435-8492
E-mail: hic-sarp@hic-sarp.org
Website: www.hic-sarp.org
Contact: Mr. Miloon Kothari or Ms. Malavika Vartak

HIC is committed to the recognition, defense, and realization of all peoples' right to a secure place to live in peace and dignity. One of its programs is HLRN, which has its coordination office in Cairo. HLRN in New Delhi administers the South Asian Regional Program (SARP), working with groups in Bangladesh, Bhutan, Burma, India, Nepal, Pakistan, Sri Lanka, and Tibet.

Through research, capacity building, and advocacy initiatives, SARP focuses on housing and land rights of people facing eviction, women's right to adequate housing, and building solidarity for children's right to housing. SARP has documented cases of housing and land rights violations and sought solutions within the human rights framework. SARP has taken its analyses and advocacy to various international bodies, including the UN, to press for better international human rights instruments.

SARP welcomes applications from volunteers interested in housing and land rights in South Asia. Volunteers must commit to working from six months to a year and should have prior experience of legal research, plus excellent writing and coordination skills. Volunteers are expected to cover all costs, although a small stipend may be provided for travel and food expenses. For more information, contact the persons listed above.

Incarnate Word Missionaries (IWM)

4503 Broadway, San Antonio, TX 78230
Tel: (210) 828-2224, ext. 228
Fax: (210) 828-9741
E-mail: gloria.drews@amormeus.org
Website: www.amormeus.org

IWM seeks a new economic, social, and political order promoting justice and solidarity. Missionaries work with homeless women and children and indigenous peoples, performing services that may include human rights work, health-care, clinic/hospice ministry, and pastoral ministry. Our missionaries serve in the US, Guatemala, Mexico, and Peru.

IWM missionaries must be at least 21 years old, in good physical and mental health, single or married without dependents, willing to commit to one year in their own country or two to three years in a country other than their own, willing to live a simple lifestyle, open to working with a preferential option for the poor, and of the Christian faith (some sites require that one be Catholic). Those who wish to serve in Latin America must have some degree of fluency in the Spanish language.

The missionary pays the cost of transportation to the orientation site, language school, and vacation travel and emergency leave, as well as any costs incurred for preexisting medical conditions. All other costs are paid by IWM.

InterConnection
(Because their web-savvy work in support of worldwide NGOs is done without leaving home, see the listing under US Voluntary Service Organizations)

International Society for Ecology and Culture (ISEC)
PO Box 9475, Berkeley, CA 94709
Tel: (510) 548-4915
Fax: (510) 548-4916
E-mail: isecca@igc.org
Website: www.isec.org.uk

ISEC is concerned with raising awareness about the root causes of today's social, environmental, and economic crises. In challenging economic globalization and conventional notions of "progress," ISEC promotes localization, thereby helping to strengthen community and restore the environment. ISEC produces books, videos, and other educational material and promotes grassroots and policy-level strategies for ecological and community renewal.

One-month farm-stays in ISEC's Ladakh Farm Project are available during July and August. Participants live and work with Ladakhi families in northern India and are exposed to both the strengths of Ladakhi traditional culture and the forces threatening to undermine it. The cost is $350, which includes room and board on the farm. Volunteers are expected to cover their own travel expenses, but financial aid is occasionally available for participants from low-income backgrounds. Ladakh is located at extremely high altitudes and requires a great deal of manual labor, so volunteers should be able to work under these conditions. ISEC does have other volunteer opportunities; contact their office at the above address for more information.

Interns for Peace (IFP)

475 Riverside Drive, 2nd Floor, New York, NY 10115
Tel: (212) 870-226
Fax: (212) 870-2119
E-mail: ifpus@mindspring.com
Website: www.internsforpeace.org

IFP is an independent, nonpolitical, community-sponsored program dedicated to building trust and respect among the Jewish and Arab citizens of Israel. Guided by field staff, interns carry out the program while receiving work experience in human relations, conflict resolution, and group facilitation. Interns take on projects in education, sports, health, the arts, community and workplace relations, and adult interest groups. Basic requirements include a knowledge of and commitment to furthering Jewish-Arab relations; a BA, BS, or an equivalent degree; proficiency in Hebrew or Arabic; a previous stay in Israel of at least six months; previous experience in community or human relations work; and a background in sports, business, teaching, health care, youth work, art, music, or community organizing. Interns are provided with housing and a monthly stipend for food, health insurance, transportation, and other daily living expenses. Interns are Jews or Arabs from Israel and abroad. Internships require a two-year commitment.

Interplast

300-B Pioneer Way, Mountain View, CA 94041-1506
Tel: (888) 467-5278
Fax: (650) 962-1619
E-mail: IPNews@interplast.org or volunteers@interplast.org
Website: www.interplast.org

Interplast is a nonprofit organization partnering with physicians in developing countries to provide free reconstructive plastic surgery for needy children and adults. Interplast coordinates support and advanced training for local surgeons and manages volunteer service programs to care for more than 3,000 impoverished patients every year. Interplast's programs provide surgeries for patients with congenital deformities (cleft lip, cleft palate) or those with severe burns, hand injuries, or other crippling injuries. Interplast's scope of services includes supporting surgeons in developing countries managing their own outreach programs, sending volunteer medical teams overseas to perform the needed surgeries and assist in skills transfer, and conducting workshops that provide advanced training in specialized skills for host country medical professionals.

Working at more than 25 different sites in over 12 countries in Africa, Central and South America, South and Southeast Asia, Interplast has provided almost 57,000 life-changing surgeries since 1969. Interplast has six surgical outreach centers in Bangladesh, Ecuador, Nepal, Peru (2), and Zambia. Plastic surgeons, pediatricians, anesthesiologists, operating room nurses, and recovery room nurses are needed in a volunteer capacity. Each team also requires a secretary/translator who provides general patient, family, and team support and performs clerical work. For more information or to fill out a volunteer application, visit the website or contact *volunteers@interplast.org*.

Jesuit Volunteer Corps (JVC)   ⚛ ⚛ ⚛

PO Box 3756, Washington, DC 20027-0256
Website: www.jesuitvolunteers.org

JVC EAST COAST:
Tel: (215) 232-0300
E-mail: jvceast@jesuitvolunteers.org

JVC MIDWEST:
Tel: (313) 345-3480
E-mail: jvcmw@jesuitvolunteers.org

JVC NORTHWEST:
Tel: (503) 335-8202
E-mail: jvcnw@jesuitvolunteers.org

JVC SOUTH:
Tel: (713) 756-5095
E-mail: jvcsouth@jesuitvolunteers.org

JVC SOUTHWEST:
Tel: (510) 653-8564
E-mail: jvcsw@jesuitvolunteers.org

JVC (INTERNATIONAL):
Tel: (202) 687-1132
E-mail: jvi@jesuitvolunteers.org

Each year JVC offers about 500 men and women the opportunity to work full time for justice and peace by serving the poor
directly and working for structural change. The challenge
to Jesuit Volunteers (JVs) is to integrate Christian faith by
working and living among the poor, living modestly in a cooperative household with other JVs, and examining the causes of
social injustice. JVs serve as teachers, counselors, nurses, social
workers, community organizers, and lawyers, and work with
the homeless, physically and mentally ill, elderly, children,
refugees, prisoners, and migrant workers. JVs serve in Belize,
Bolivia, Chile, Haiti, the Marshall Islands, Micronesia, Nepal,
Nicaragua, Peru, South Africa, Tanzania, and the US.

JVC welcomes women and men from diverse backgrounds.
Applicants must have a Christian motivation, be 21 or older,

have a college degree or applicable work experience, and be without dependents. There is a particular need for applicants competent in Spanish.

Domestic placements are for one year and begin in August. International placements require a two-year commitment and also begin in August. JVC provides room and board, health insurance, a small personal stipend, local support teams, workshops and retreats during the year, transportation home at the end of the term of service, and an active alumni association. Applications are accepted January through July with preference given to applications received before March 1. The deadline for international applicants is February 1.

Jewish Volunteer Corps (JVS)
American Jewish World Service (AJWS)
45 West 36th Street, 10th Floor, New York, NY 10018
Tel: (800) 889-7146 or (212) 736-2597
Fax: (212) 736-3463
E-mail: volunteer@ajws.org
Website: www.ajws.org

AJWS is a nonprofit international development agency providing nonsectarian humanitarian assistance to communities throughout the developing world. AJWS works exclusively with local nongovernmental organizations in the fields of health care, sustainable agriculture, microcredit, and education. Through the Jewish Volunteer Corps, AJWS places professional Jewish men and women on short-term volunteer consulting assignments with their partners in the developing world. JVC volunteers provide technical assistance and training to the host organization while experiencing a new country and culture from the inside.

The International Jewish College Corps (IJCC) is a summer program for college students that interweaves in-depth exploration of international development; study of Jewish texts and traditions relating to social justice, human rights, religious pluralism, and racial tolerance; and humanitarian service in hands-on volunteer projects in the developing world and Israel. For more information, please contact through e-mail address.

Joint Assistance Center, Inc. (JAC)
PO Box 6082, San Pablo, CA 94806-0082
Tel: (510) 237-8331
Fax: (510) 217-6671
E-mail: jacusa@juno.com
Website: www.jacusa.org

JAC is a nongovernmental voluntary organization headquartered in Haryana State in the outskirts of Delhi, India. It coordinates conferences and training in various parts of India on disaster preparedness and works in liaison with groups, individuals, and small grassroots projects throughout the country, focusing on such areas as community, welfare, health, education, youth development, and agricultural training. JAC welcomes volunteers from around the world to participate in the work of its partner organizations. Short-term projects (minimum one month) can involve sanitation, construction, agriculture, the environment, public health, or literacy; long-term projects (three months or more) are similar to the short-term ones but allow for greater depth.

JAC programs run year-round. Arrangements must be made at least 30 days in advance of the volunteer's arrival in India. Volunteers participate in an orientation program in New Delhi before departing for their assigned village. In New Delhi volunteers stay at a JAC-maintained dormitory; accommodations at work camps are in homes, schools, or other public buildings. The registration fee is $50; the cost for one month is $230, airfare not included. For a long-term placement, the fee is $550 for the first three months and $125 for each month thereafter, airfare not included. JAC also coordinates volunteer programs with organizations in Bangladesh, Nepal, and South Korea. Send a self-addressed stamped envelope to the address above or follow the links from JAC's home page to find out more.

Los Niños

287 G Street, Chula Vista, CA 91910
Tel: (619) 426-9110
Fax: (619) 426-6664
E-mail: info@losninosinternational.org
Website: www.losninosinternational.org

Los Niños supports long-term community development projects along the US-Mexico border, and works with high schools and universities in Canada and the US. Program areas include nutrition, ecology, microcredit, cross-cultural issues, and education, and are designed to promote self-reliance and social awareness. Los Niños offers long-term volunteer opportunities to help assist in these programs. Volunteers are expected to make a minimum commitment of one year. Interested candidates should send a resume to the above e-mail address. Los Niños has no religious or political affiliations.

(Also listed under Alternative Travel and Study Overseas)

MADRE / Sisters without Borders ⊗

121 West 27th Street, Room 301, New York, NY 10001
Tel: (212) 627-0444
Fax (212) 675-3704
E-mail: volunteers@madre.org
Website: www.madre.org

Through our volunteer program, Sisters without Borders, MADRE arranges for culturally competent, skilled professionals to work with women and children and provide assistance to staff and community leaders at our sister organizations in Guatemala, Kenya, Mexico, Nicaragua, Palestine, and Peru. Volunteers help strengthen community-based women's organizations that work to meet immediate needs for women and families while promoting long-term change for social justice and human rights. Our volunteers cover their own travel costs and living expenses and must have credentials and experience in the field in which they would like to work. Fluency in Spanish is necessary for all countries in Latin America. English-language skills are sufficient for Kenya, while Arabic-language skills are preferred but not required for Palestine. A time commitment of at least three to six months is required.

MADRE places volunteer skilled professionals in these areas:

• Human rights law and advocacy: trainings and popular education in women's human rights, labor rights, the rights of indigenous peoples, and sexual and reproductive rights; human rights documentation; and international and humanitarian law

• Women's and children's health: trauma, community mental health, substance-abuse counseling, child psychology, general medicine, nursing, midwifery, dentistry, and social work

• Media and computer literacy: video and radio production, journalism, photography, computer technology, web design and Internet skills

• Education and the arts: popular education workshops and human rights trainings, creative arts workshops and programming, weaving and sewing, primary and secondary education, and English-language instruction

• Food security and sustainable development: agriculture, organic farming/gardening, and sustainable development

• Administration and organizational development: administration and office management, organizational and program development, project management, fund-raising, budget management and planning, and accounting

Maryknoll Lay Missioners

Maryknoll Mission Association of the Faithful, Inc.
PO Box 307, Maryknoll, NY 10545-0307
Tel: (800) 818-5276
Fax: (914) 762-7031
E-mail: admissions@mklm.org
Website: http://laymissioners.maryknoll.org

Maryknoll Mission Association of the Faithful, popularly known as Maryknoll Lay Missioners, is part of the Maryknoll mission family. It is a Catholic community of lay, religious, and ordained people, including families and children. Maryknoll Lay Missioners participate in the mission of Jesus, working in cross-cultural ministries in order to create a more just world in solidarity with marginalized and oppressed peoples. Missioners come from a wide range of professional and educational backgrounds and may serve in the fields of health (including direct service to persons with AIDS), education, community organizing, grassroots economic development, and formation of faith communities. Mission sites are located in Brazil, Bolivia, Cambodia, Chile, East Timor, El Salvador, Kenya, Mexico, Nepal, Panama, Peru, Tanzania, Thailand, Venezuela, Vietnam, Zimbabwe, and on the US-Mexico border.

Medair

Chemin du Croset 9, 1024 Ecublens, Switzerland
Tel: 011 (41 21) 694-3535
Fax: 011 (41 21) 694-3540
E-mail: personnel@medair.org
Website: www.medair.org
Contact: Christina Bregy, Recruitment Officer

Based in Switzerland, Medair is a disaster-relief program currently addressing needs of certain countries in the Middle East (Afghanistan and Iran) and a number of African countries (Angola, Congo, Liberia, Madagascar, Sudan, and Zimbabwe). Inspired by its Christian ethos, Medair seeks to reduce human suffering through its relief and rehabilitation projects. Though mitigating "after the fact" in catastrophic situations, Medair also works with communities through Disaster Preparedness and Disaster Mitigation activities to prevent the most damaging results of a recurrence.

Potential volunteers between 25 and 55 years of age should have at least one year's professional experience in a field relevant to a Medair job profile (titled Administrator, Engineer,

Health Professional, Logistician, and Manager, they are available in downloadable pdf files from the website). Placements range between one and a half to two years in length. Volunteers are responsible for covering the cost of the mandatory "Relief and Rehabilitation Orientation Course" (€ 535) and their first flight to the field. Medair covers other costs and provides a modest stipend. For detailed information consult the website.

Mennonite Central Committee (MCC)

PO Box 500, Akron, PA 17501-0500
Tel: (717) 859-1151
Fax: (717) 859-2171
E-mail: mailbox@mcc.org
Website: www.mcc.org

MCC is the cooperative relief, service, and peace agency of the Mennonite and Brethren in Christ churches in North America. Currently just over 1,200 persons serve in agriculture, health, education, social services, and community development fields in 55 countries, including the US and Canada. Qualifications depend on assignment. Transportation, living expenses, and a small stipend are provided. MCC asks that volunteers be Christian, actively involved in a church congregation, and in agreement with MCC's nonviolent principles. Placements are for three years overseas or two years in North America. For a list of current assignment openings, visit the website.

Middle East Children's Alliance (MECA)
(See listing under Alternative Travel and Study Overseas)

MondoChallenge
Galiford Building, Gayton Road, Milton Malsor,
    Northampton NN7 3AB, United Kingdom
Tel: 011 (44 160) 485-8225
Fax: 011 (44 160) 485-9323
E-mail: info@mondochallenge.org
Website: www.mondochallenge.org
Contact: Davina Jeffery

MondoChallenge is a midsized NGO based in England that matches motivated volunteers (with particular emphasis in teaching or business) with short-term community-generated projects in Chile, Gambia, India, Kenya, Nepal, Sri Lanka, and Tanzania. The volunteer placement ranges from two to six months in length (average is three) and is ideal for persons of various ages seeking to make a positive impact (and are ready to be similarly impacted). Potential volunteers over 18 need only have an interest in education to work on many projects, including HIV/AIDS awareness and support for affected communities. Those interested in business development projects are asked to have five years' experience. The average three-month placement currently costs volunteers the equivalent of £900 (though costs may be less for volunteers not based in the UK).

Network in Solidarity with the People of Guatemala (NISGUA)
Guatemala Accompaniment Project (GAP)

1830 Connecticut Avenue NW, Washington, DC 20009
Tel: (202) 265-8713
Fax: (202) 223-8221
Email: nisguagap@igc.org
Website: www.nisgua.org
Contact: Jennifer Morley, US Program Coordinator

NISGUA's Guatemala Accompaniment Project creates a non-violent response to the injustices and violence suffered by Guatemalan communities, survivors of the 36-year-long civil war, and grassroots organizations. Through NISGUA placements, volunteers live side by side with individuals, organizations, and communities, in an effort to deter human rights violations. These volunteers, known as accompaniers, monitor the situation and alert the international community to abuses. The accompaniers' presence provides a measure of security and creates space for Guatemalan communities and organizations networking to defend their rights.

Volunteers commit to at minimum six months of service and are at least 21. Potential accompaniers should have an

understanding of the history of Central America/US relationships and the current situation in Guatemala; an understanding of accompaniment and nonviolence, and a willingness to
continue developing that understanding; previous experience
in Latin America (strongly preferred); a proficiency in Spanish
or the ability to develop it with six weeks of study; the ability to
document and analyze; cultural sensitivity; excellent judgment
skills; physical stamina and good health; awareness of security
issues and willingness to work in a situation that might involve
some risk; and US or Canadian citizenship, or a strong connection to a community in the US or Canada. Accompaniers must
also successfully complete the GAP training.

Estimated expenses for the volunteer are from \$520 to
\$2,270 but NISGUA does provide training on grassroots fund-
raising techniques. Accompaniers in the field receive a stipend
and other program-related costs are covered. We can sometimes
accommodate people with physical disabilities. Visit the website for further details on accompaniment, qualifications, and
finances.

Nicaragua Network

1247 E Street SE, Washington, DC 20003
Tel: (202) 544-9355
Fax: (202) 544-9359
E-mail: nicanet@afgj.org
Website: www.nicanet.org

For a quarter of a century the Nicaragua Network has been a
leading organization in the US committed to social and economic justice for Nicaragua and Latin America, based upon
respect for sovereignty and self-determination. The Network
advocates for sound US foreign policies that respect human
rights and international law. The Nicaragua Network provides
information and organizing tools to a network of 200 solidarity, sister-city, and peace and justice committees across the US.
Publications include the Nicaragua Network Hotline, the

Nicaragua News Service, the Nicaragua Monitor, and occasional monographs. The Network organizes speaking tours of Nicaraguans in the US and study tours and volunteer brigades to Nicaragua. Some important current campaigns are confronting water privatization, debt cancellation for Nicaragua and other poor countries, and radical change of IMF/World Bank measures. We also have campaigns in support of unemployed coffee workers, banana workers, labor organizing in the Free Trade Zones, indigenous rights, and the efforts of Nicaraguan environmental organizations.

(Also listed under Alternative Travel and Study Overseas)

Nuestros Pequeños Hermanos International (NPHI)

Apdo. Postal 333 (Regular Mail) or Calle Nacional No. 44
    (FedEx or UPS), Cuernavaca, Morelos 62100, Mexico
Tel: 011 (52) 777-311-2654
Fax: 011 (52) 777-311-2655
E-mail: rhyland@nphi.org
Website: www.nphamigos.org
Contact: Ryan Hyland, NPHI Information Officer

NPHI provides homes for orphaned and abandoned children in Bolivia, the Dominican Republic, El Salvador, Guatemala, Haiti, Honduras, Mexico, Nicaragua, and Peru. The mission is to provide shelter, food, clothing, health care, and education in a Christian family environment based on unconditional acceptance and love. Volunteers from North America and Europe should be at least 21 years old, with a working knowledge of Spanish (French or Creole for Haiti) and experience working with children. Volunteers must commit to one year of service. There are no fees for the NPHI program, but transportation and personal expenses are not covered. The website provides current information as well as an online volunteer application.

Operation Crossroads Africa
34 Mount Morris Park West, New York, NY 10027
Tel: (212) 289-1949
Fax: (212) 289-2526
E-mail: oca@igc.org
Website: http://operationcrossroadsafrica.org

Established in 1957, Operation Crossroads Africa oversees two volunteer programs: the Africa program, which annually supports from 15 to 20 work projects in Africa; and the Diaspora program, which focuses on Brazil because of its large Afro-Brazilian population. Crossroads programs run in the following African countries: Benin, Botswana, Burkina Faso, Ethiopia, The Gambia, Ghana, Kenya, Lesotho, Malawi, Mali, Namibia, Senegal, South Africa, Tanzania, and Uganda. The Crossroads summer consists of three orientation days in New York City, six weeks of service on a rural project, and one week of travel in the host country. All Crossroads ventures are community initiated, and volunteers live and work with hosts who have designed the project. Among the possible assignments are construction of community facilities, public health drives, reforestation, and teaching. Specialized skills in medicine, construction, or local languages are welcome but not necessary. The fee for participation is $3,500, exclusive of transportation to and from New York. Crossroads provides fund-raising advice and a limited number of partial scholarships based on need. Successful participation requires an interest in Africa and the Diaspora, strong communication skills, a desire to establish meaningful contact with people of other cultures, and a willingness to respect different beliefs and values. Many volunteers have been able to arrange academic credit for their service with Crossroads.

Peace Brigades International (PBI)

428 8th Street SE, Washington, DC 20003
Tel: (202) 544-3765
Fax: (202) 544-3766
E-mail: info@pbiusa.org
Website: www.peacebrigades.org

Founded in 1981, PBI pioneered and practices an effective approach to human rights protection known as protective accompaniment. PBI fields teams of international volunteers trained in nonviolence to accompany individuals and organizations facing death threats as a result of their work on behalf of human rights and social justice. PBI's work—based on the principals of nonviolence, nonpartisanship, and noninterference in the affairs of the groups they accompany—also includes intensive networking with local, national, and international officials; distribution of human rights information to the international community; and public education in the US and other countries.

PBI currently has projects in Colombia, Guatemala, Indonesia, and Mexico. Prospective volunteers attend a seven- to ten-day training before final selections are made. Participants must be at least 25 years old and willing to commit to one year of field service. Candidates for our Latin America projects must be fluent in Spanish, and candidates for Indonesia must be conversant in or willing to learn Bahasa Indonesian. Upon acceptance, PBI covers travel, housing, food, health insurance, and other work-related expenses, in addition to a modest monthly stipend.

Peacework

209 Otey Street, Blacksburg, VA 24060-7426
Tel: (800) 272-5519 or (540) 953-1376
Fax: (540) 953-0300
E-mail: mail@peacework.org
Website: www.peacework.org

Peacework manages short-term volunteer service projects around the world in cooperation with indigenous relief and development organizations. Projects are normally organized for groups, which can include persons from colleges, universities, progressive churches, and civic, medical, or other professional organizations. Orientation and interaction with the host community is a vital part of the program. Volunteers may provide valuable hands-on assistance building houses, repairing orphanages, schools, and health facilities. Volunteers may also provide direct medical services, or be involved in health education, school tutoring, environmental efforts, wildlife conservation, and other projects with a local community and self-development focus. International experience, building skills, volunteer service, and foreign language proficiency are helpful but not required. Groups with a genuine interest in humanitarian service are invited to participate. Project locations include: Belize, Costa Rica, the Czech Republic, the Dominican Republic, Honduras, Mexico, Nicaragua, Russia, Vietnam, and the US. Typical costs range from $500 to $1,200 plus airfare. Limited scholarships are available. Contact Peacework for information about locations, projects, dates, and budgets.

Plenty International

PO Box 394, Summertown, TN 38483
Tel/Fax: (931) 964-4864
E-mail: plenty@plenty.org
Website: www.plenty.org

Founded in 1974, Plenty promotes the cooperative exchange of appropriate village-scale technologies, skills, and resources between people worldwide. Special focus is on projects to assist indigenous peoples. Volunteer placements are limited and are based primarily in Belize. Volunteers must pay all travel and living expenses. Long-term volunteers (three months or more) skilled in organic agriculture, midwifery, nutrition, or sustainable energy are most often used. Check the website for a listing of current volunteer opportunities.

Quest—Volunteers for Haiti

4602 Clemson Road, College Park, MD 20704
Tel: (301) 927-7118
E-mail: collegeparkrjm@aol.com
Website: www.rjm-us.org
Contact: Sr. Rita Ricker, RJM

Quest—Volunteers for Haiti, a volunteer program sponsored by the Religious of Jesus and Mary, offers year-long and summer opportunities in Gros Morne and Jean Rabel, Haiti. Volunteers share simple living with one or two Religious of Jesus and Mary while daily serving the poor in a variety of social and educational ministries. Orientation, room and board, medical insurance, a monthly stipend, retreats, and daily transportation are provided. Volunteers must pay their own transportation at the beginning and end of term to and from the Haiti site.

Right To Play (RTP)

65 Queen Street West, Suite 1900, Box 64, Toronto,
    Ontario M5H 2M5, Canada
Tel: (416) 498-1922, ext. 225
Fax: (416) 498-1942
E-mail: recruitment@righttoplay.com
Website: www.righttoplay.com

What distinguishes RTP from other nonprofits working with worldwide communities for sustainable development is its focus on athletic programs. Based in Toronto but fielding programs in Africa, the Middle East, and both South and Southeast Asia, RTP uses sports for youth development and community building projects. RTP seeks persons in their mid-20s and older who have international experience plus some background either in adult education, project management, sports and recreation, or child development. By committing to a one- to two-year placement, RTP volunteers have time to assess how their work has made a difference in a community. Though projects can often be physically demanding, RTP has placed disabled volunteers and welcomes their applications.

Volunteers cover the cost of a passport, a police criminal record check, and in-field food and social expenses. Besides training, in-field accommodations and transportation, visas, and vaccinations, RTP provides a volunteer stipend that amounts to $8,000 for a 12-month placement.

Service Civil International (SCI)
International Voluntary Service (IVS)
US Branch of Service Civil International
5474 Walnut Level Road, Crozet, VA 22932
Tel/Fax: (206) 350-6585
E-mail: info@sci-ivs.org
Website: www.sci-ivs.org

SCI is a voluntary service organization and peace movement with 37 branches worldwide. Founded in 1920, SCI organizes international volunteer projects all over the world in the belief that if people with different backgrounds and cultures learn to cooperate and work together peace can be the result. SCI organizes short-term projects—called work camps—and long-term (1 to 12 months) projects in Africa, Asia, Europe, Latin America, and the US. Volunteers work on environmental, social, solidarity, and construction/maintenance projects and must be at least 16 years of age for the US, 18 for Europe, and 21 for all others. Volunteers pay travel expenses and receive the benefit of room and board and accident insurance while on the project. The application fee for US camps is $65 and $175 for most overseas projects. Most camps occur from July to September and last two to three weeks.

Servicio Internacional para la Paz (SIPAZ)
PO Box 3584, Chico, CA 95927
Tel/Fax: (530) 892-0662
E-mail: info@sipaz.org
In Mexico: Calle Dr. Navarro No. 20-b, San Cristóbal de Las Casas,
     CP 29220 Chiapas, Mexico
E-mail: chiapas@sipaz.org

Organized at the invitation of Mexican church and human rights groups, SIPAZ is a coalition of North American, Latin American, and European organizations dedicated to supporting the peace process in Chiapas. SIPAZ seeks long-term volunteers to help carry out its work. Tasks include developing and maintaining relationships with groups and individuals concerned in the conflict, monitoring both formal talks and independent initiatives, preparing updates and analysis on the ongoing peace process, designing workshops on nonviolence, and assisting with presence and accompaniment duties. Prospective volunteers must be fluent in Spanish, 23 years or older, and have prior international work experience. Candidates should be committed to nonviolence and comfortable working with faith-based groups. A commitment of at least one year is required.

Toledo Eco-Tourism Association (TEA)

PO Box 45, Punta Gorda, Belize
Tel: 011 (501) 722-2096
Fax: 011 (501) 722-2199
E-mail: ttea@btl.net or pabloack@hotmail.com
Website: www.ecoclub.com/toledo/
Contact: Pablo Ack, TEA Secretary

TEA works with nine indigenous communities in the areas of ecotourism, rainforest conservation, and sustainable development. The association has been active since 1990. Founded in 1996, the Punta Gorda Conservation Committee (PGCC) is an urban group seeking to establish ecotourist sites on what remains of public lands around Punta Gorda. The sites will be run by and for the benefit of local people. Volunteers have worked as instructors in training for office operation, trail development, guide training, arts and crafts development, grant writing, and media. A major current project is the establishment of community conservation areas for 19 villages for which a grant is pending with United Nations Development Program. Volunteers must cover all expenses, including transportation, room, and board. Participant costs average $20 per day or $400 per month. Belizeans speak English. Volunteers should commit to a stay of three to six months. For further information, check the website.

Visions in Action

2710 Ontario Road NW, Washington, DC 20009
Tel: (202) 625-7402
E-mail: visions@visionsinaction.org
Website: www.visionsinaction.org

Visions in Action is a nonprofit organization that offers six-month and one-year volunteer positions in Mexico, South Africa, Tanzania, and Uganda. Positions are available with non-profit development organizations, research institutes, health clinics, community groups, and the media. The program features an orientation with language study followed by a home-stay in a local community. Volunteers for long-term programs must be at least 20 years old and have two years of college or equivalent work experience. A college degree is beneficial but not a requirement. The program is open to people of any nationality. Married couples are also encouraged to apply. Program fees cover housing, health insurance, medical evacuation insurance, orientation, local staff and in-country support, program administration, and a stipend. Program fees vary by country. The average cost is $4,000.

For those seeking short-term volunteer placement, Visions in Action also offers in Mexico and Tanzania a seven-week summer program and a three-week winter program. For short-term programs, 18 is the minimum age.

Voluntarios Solidarios
Fellowship of Reconciliation (FOR)
Task Force on Latin America and the Caribbean

2017 Mission Street, Suite 305, San Francisco, CA 94110
Tel: (415) 495-6334
Fax: (415) 495-5628
E-mail: volfor@igc.org
Website: www.forusa.org

Voluntarios Solidarios places volunteers with groups in Latin America (Argentina, Bolivia, Chile, Colombia, Ecuador, Mexico, Paraguay, and Peru) and the Caribbean (main island of Puerto Rico and Vieques) that are engaged in nonviolence education, human rights documentation, and advocacy efforts with the regions' poor majority. Each volunteer's work is shaped by the needs of the host organization. Common needs include translation of publications, support of peace actions, technical assistance in carpentry, computer operation, recycling, assistance with human welfare service, child and elderly care projects, and conflict resolution. Volunteers must be self-funded, at least 21 years old, and functional in Spanish. Placements range in length from three months to two years.

Voluntary Service Overseas (VSO) Canada

806-151 Slater Street, Ottawa, Ontario K1P 5H3, Canada
Tel: (888) 876-2911
Fax: (613) 234-1444
E-mail: inquiry@vsocan.org
Website: www.vsocan.org

VSO Canada is a government-funded international development agency that through its volunteers works with local partners to reduce poverty and empower individuals to make lasting positive change in their communities. VSO currently sponsors programs in 35 countries throughout Africa and Asia, and including many Pacific Island nations. Applicants should be between 19 and 68 years of age and be citizens of Canada or the US, or be Canadian Permanent Residents. Placements overseas are usually two years in length but shorter terms may be available—particularly for those in the VSO Business Partnership Program. VSO asks that potential volunteers have relevant qualifications and experience in the fields in which they will be working (one-year experience for NetCorps and two or more for the Volunteer Sending Program). VSO welcomes applications from people with disabilities, and strives to enable them to fully participate.

VSO offers a comprehensive package of training and support for its volunteers. Included in the orientation is six weeks' language training for those planning to teach English; volunteers in other programs customarily receive ten weeks' training. Most key volunteer expenses are covered by VSO, including overseas accommodations and return airfare. To help defray the cost of equipment purchases and incidental expenses, VSO provides predeparture, in-country, and resettlement grants to all volunteers. While in the placement, volunteers receive a living allowance or stipend. Because the VSO Canada program has many facets, potential applicants should thoroughly research the extensive website.

Volunteer Missionary Movement (VMM)

5980 West Loomis Road, Greendale, WI 53129
Tel: (414) 423-8660
Fax: (414) 423-8964
E-mail: vmm@vmmusa.org
Website: www.vmmusa.org

VMM is a nonsectarian international community of Christians, with an origin in the Catholic tradition, which seeks, by sharing resources, skills, and lives, to challenge oppressive unjust structures and promote equality, respect, and dignity. VMM sponsors locally initiated programs in Africa (Ethiopia, Kenya, South Africa, Sudan, Tanzania, Uganda, and Zambia), Central America (El Salvador and Guatemala), and the US. The term of placement is a minimum of two years, and is open to anyone 23 years of age or older who can dedicate the time to serve "God's poor and marginalized." VMM asks potential volunteers to have at least one year's work experience, though some placements do require a technical or bachelor's degree. Where the project partner is amenable, VMM will work to place a volunteer with a disability.

VMM covers the cost of health insurance, training, travel to and from the mission site, language school, living stipend, and resettlement allowance. The project partner typically takes care of room and board. Out of a total placement cost of $17,000, the volunteer is expected to raise $6,000. VMM helps the volunteer develop a fund-raising plan to make it simple.

(Also listed under US Voluntary Service Organizations)

Volunteers for Peace, Inc. (VFP)
1034 Tiffany Road, Belmont, VT 05730
Tel: (802) 259-2759
Fax: (802) 259-2922
E-mail: vfp@vfp.org
Website: www.vfp.org

VFP recruits volunteers for over 2,500 work camps in 80 different countries (located in North, Central, and South America; Asia; Africa; Europe; as well as some Pacific Islands). At a work camp, 10 to 20 people from five or more countries join together for two to three weeks to support community projects in construction, restoration, environmental work, social services, agriculture, and archaeology. In 2002 VFP exchanged over 1,300 volunteers. Volunteers arrange their own travel and pay a registration fee of $200, which covers room and board for the duration of most programs. Volunteers can participate in multiple camps in the same or different countries. Call, write, or e-mail VFP for a free newsletter, which includes many reports and photos from their programs.

(Also listed under Resources)

VIA (formerly Volunteers in Asia)
PO Box 20266, Stanford, CA 94309
Tel: (650) 723-3228
Fax: (650) 725-1805
E-mail: info@viaprograms.org
Website: www.viaprograms.org

For over 40 years VIA has been facilitating cross-cultural exchange between Americans of all ages and partner institutions and organizations in Asia. Each year VIA places approximately 40 volunteers in China, Indonesia, and Vietnam. We offer six-to eight-week summer programs for college undergraduates in addition to one- and two-year placements for college graduates of all ages. While most VIA volunteers work as English teachers, we also offer English resource posts with local nonprofit organizations. Programs are open to native English speakers who are either US citizens or residents. Program fees range from $975 to $1,975 and cover round-trip airfare, insurance, predeparture and in-country training, field and home support, and housing. VIA offers need-based scholarships. One- and two-year volunteers receive a living stipend from their hosting institutions.

Witness for Peace (WFP) $ 💱 🏘

707 8th Street SE, Suite 100, Washington, DC 20003
Tel: (202) 547-6112
Fax: (202) 547-6103
E-mail: witness@witnessforpeace.org
Website: www.witnessforpeace.org

Volunteers with WFP work with communities in Colombia, Cuba, Mexico, and Nicaragua, making a two-year commitment. Long-term volunteers document human rights abuses, study the effects of North American foreign and economic policies on the region, provide sociopolitical analyses of domestic affairs, facilitate short-term delegations of North Americans, and stand with the people in the spirit of international awareness and the ethos of nonviolence as a means for positive social change. Volunteers must be US citizens and fluent in Spanish. Volunteers pay costs of roundtrip airfare and attempt to raise $1,000 for WFP to help cover living expenses. WFP provides training, room and board, medical, and a monthly stipend. WPF is an interfaith organization.

WorkingAbroad Projects

PO Box 454, Flat 1, Brighton BN1 3ZS, East Sussex, United Kingdom
Tel/Fax: 011 (44 0) 1273-711-406
E-mail: info@workingabroad.com
Website: www.workingabroad.com

WorkingAbroad Projects is a nonprofit that provides volunteer assistance to small-scale organizations on request. The aim is to create small, independent, and effective projects that directly engage grassroots organizations in these focus areas: cultural development, earth restoration, permaculture, indigenous rights, and traditional arts and music. WorkingAbroad Projects has current programs in Costa Rica, the Netherlands Antilles, and Iceland. Volunteers should be at least 18 years old and culturally aware. The cost for the two-month program ranges from $859 to $1,480, which includes room and board, materials, training, and local transportation. Check the website for detailed program descriptions and updates.

(Also listed under Resources)

World Bridges (WB)

1203 Preservation Park, Suite 300, Oakland, CA 94612
Tel: (510) 271-8286
Fax: (510) 451-2996
E-mail: info@world-bridges.org
Website: www.world-bridges.org

WB's mission is to promote peace and justice by creating opportunities for diverse young people from low-income backgrounds to collaborate, raise awareness, and take action —locally and globally. Through leadership development, participatory trainings, and international exchanges, WB provides a continuum of experiences that nurture personal growth and empower participants to build alliances across communities and cultures.

The Leadership Exchange Program supports diverse youth in the US—primarily from low-income backgrounds—in gaining the experience, knowledge, and skills required to be effective, globally minded leaders in multicultural and international environments. Through unique service-learning and alliance-building activities, participants gain understanding of the US role in global affairs and of their individual connections to the global community.

WorldTeach, Inc.

Center for International Development
Harvard University
79 John F. Kennedy Street, Cambridge, MA 02138
Tel: (800) 483-2240 or (617) 495-5527
Fax: (617) 495-1599
E-mail: info@worldteach.org
Website: www.worldteach.org

WorldTeach is a private, nonprofit organization based at the
Center for International Development at Harvard University.
Founded in 1986, WorldTeach provides opportunities for individuals to make a meaningful contribution to international
education by living and working as volunteer teachers in developing countries.

Volunteers teach English for 2 to 12 months to students of a
variety of ages (depending on the country). Currently, teachers
are needed in Chile, China, Costa Rica, Ecuador, the Marshall
Islands, Namibia, and Poland. A bachelor's degree (or equivalent) is required for long-term teaching assignments; volunteers must be 18 years or older for summer programs. No
previous language or teaching experience is necessary.

Room and board are provided during the period of service
for all volunteers; volunteers in long-term programs also
receive a small monthly living allowance. The program fee for
WorldTeach varies by country, ranging from $1,000 to $5,990.
Some countries are able to cover most of the cost of recruiting,
placing, training, and supporting volunteer teachers; others
must rely on volunteers to contribute or fund-raise the cost of
their placement and support. By requesting that volunteers help
fund their service overseas, WorldTeach is able to provide volunteer educators to countries that would not otherwise be able
to afford qualified teachers. Program fees cover predeparture
preparation (including visa), international airfare, insurance,
training and orientation, an in-country field director, and after-
service support and networking. Student loans may be deferred
during the term of service.

Applications are accepted on a rolling admissions basis and may be printed from the WorldTeach website or requested by contacting the WorldTeach admissions office.

Molly Moran, Volunteer, WorldTeach

My experience in Namibia has been one that I will never forget. Nothing is ever routine. The only constant is that every day offers new surprises and challenges.

I believe I have learned more about life from the children I teach than they have learned from me. Our cultures are so different and yet the basics are the same. You smile when you are happy, cry when you are sad, and eat when you are hungry. The smiles that we exchange numerous times a day mean more to them than a brand new pair of Nikes! I have made wonderful friends here, whom I will never forget, and hope to continue to learn from them and carry on our friendships wherever we may be. As long as you have an open mind and an open heart, everything else falls into place.

Young Adult Volunteer Program

Presbyterian Church (USA)
Mission Service Recruitment Office
100 Witherspoon Street, Louisville, KY 40202
Tel: (888) 728-7228, ext. 2530
Website: www.pcusa.org/msr

The Young Adult Volunteer Program of the Presbyterian Church (USA) is an opportunity for persons between the ages of 19 and 30 to explore their call to the work of Jesus Christ. This one-year program is an opportunity to experience both mission service and mission learning. Each program site shares common components that enhance the participants' experience: orientation, service, prayer, Bible study and spiritual development, and an end-of-term reentry conference. While sharing these program elements, each site uniquely challenges the participants to explore their relationship to the church and their ministry in a broken world.

Sites in other countries include Argentina, Egypt, Great Britain, Guatemala, Hungary, India, Kenya, Northern Ireland, the Philippines, and Thailand. Current US sites are (southeast) Alaska, Atlanta GA, Cincinnati OH, Hollywood CA, Miami FL, Nashville TN, Santa Cruz CA, Seattle WA, Tucson AZ, Wapato WA, and West Yellowstone MT.

The preferential application deadline is February 1 for service beginning in August and September of the same year. Funding for the year is shared by the Presbyterian Church (USA), supporting congregations or presbyteries, and the volunteer. Partial payment of outstanding student loans is available.

5

US Voluntary Service
Organizations

Working overseas is not the only way to gain community development experience. In many areas of the US, people face conditions of poverty similar to those found in other countries. Voluntary service in the US can offer a low-cost opportunity for building solid credentials toward a career in community development.

One of the best resources for domestic volunteering may well be your local yellow pages, under Social Service Organizations. Here are some organizations that recruit nationally and perform admirable work.

Association of Community Organizations for　§
Reform Now (ACORN)
972 Broad Street, 7th Floor, Newark, NJ 07102
Tel: (800) 796-6830 or (646) 721-0539
E-mail: acornrecruit1@acorn.org
Website: www.acorn.org
Contact: Allison Faelnar, National Recruiter

ACORN is a neighborhood-based, multiracial membership organization of low-income families working to gain power within institutions that affect their everyday lives. Volunteers work as grassroots organizers throughout the US. They receive a salary and must commit to one year of service. A working knowledge of Spanish and previous organizing experience are preferred, but not required.

(Also listed under International Volunteer Service Organizations)

Bikes Not Bombs (BNB)
59 Amory Street, Suite 103, Roxbury, MA 02119
Tel: (617) 442-0004
Fax: (617) 445-2439
E-mail: mail@bikesnotbombs.org
Website: www.bikesnotbombs.org

BNB is a nonprofit grassroots development and solidarity organization that uses bicycles for development work overseas and also for youth programs and community environmental action in the Boston area. BNB helps local groups form ecologically viable bicycle workshops and related projects in Central America, the Caribbean, and Africa. These projects have involved the collecting of over 20,000 donated bicycles and tons of parts that are being reused in Nicaragua, Haiti, the Dominican Republic, and El Salvador. BNB is currently sending bikes and parts to the Maya Pedal organization (Guatemala), the Village Bicycle Project (Ghana), and a new bike shop and youth program in Diepsloot, South Africa. In a new venture BNB's local youth Earn-A-Bike program—where youth learn mechanics and riding skills while rebuilding a bicycle of their own—is being replicated in Ghana and South Africa. Besides bicycle shipments, BNB provides technical assistance, training, tools, and sometimes financing for these projects.

In the Boston area, BNB runs many youth programs, including Earn-A-Bike. Interns can work in Boston with youth programs, event planning, transportation and environmental activism, bike mechanics, or computer and web issues. Experienced bilingual mechanics with business or alternative technology skills, or youth with mechanical skills, are occasionally placed overseas to assist projects, launch bike shops, or run Earn-A-Bike programs. Every February BNB conducts mechanics classes for adults who, after teaching youth in Boston, may qualify to work overseas.

(Also listed under International Voluntary Service Organizations)

Buddhist Alliance for Social Engagement (BASE)
PO Box 3470, Berkeley, CA 94703
Tel: (510) 655-6169
Fax: (510) 655-1369
E-mail: base@bpf.org
Website: www.bpf.org/base.html

BASE is a program of the Buddhist Peace Fellowship, begun in the San Francisco Bay Area in 1995. BASE provides a structure for a group of volunteers to spend six months in service/social change work combined with intensive Buddhist practice. Placements include work in soup kitchens, shelters, hospices, urban community garden projects, and social justice organizations.

BASE volunteers meet regularly for study of Engaged Buddhism, meditation, and discussion and support. Applicants must have service, group, and meditation experience. In addition to Bay Area BASE groups, the program has expanded to include groups in Boston MA, Boulder CO, Santa Cruz CA, and Arcata CA.

Casa de Proyecto Libertad (PL)
113 North First Street, Harlingen, TX 78550
Tel: (956) 425-9552
Fax: (956) 425-8249

PL promotes and defends the human rights of the border communities in South Texas through immigration legal services, advocacy, and community organizing. PL's legal programs include the NACARA Project, the Unaccompanied Minors in

Detention Project, the Violence Against Women Act (VAWA) Project, and representation in immigration court and with the INS. PL works with political asylum, temporary protected status, naturalization, and family visa applicants. PL also facilitates the emergence of grassroots community organizations whose members are impacted by immigration laws and enforcement policies. PL provides human rights trainings as one step toward self-determination and social change. There are volunteer opportunities in the legal and community organizing programs for those who speak Spanish and are sensitive about cultural differences. Volunteers pay their own expenses, but some assistance may be available.

Catholic Worker Movement (CW)

The Catholic Worker
36 East 1st Street, New York, NY 10003
Website: www.catholicworker.org

The Catholic Worker Movement has 165 locations throughout the US and Canada, as well as 16 international locations. There is no national Catholic Worker headquarters; however, for a copy of or subscription to The Catholic Worker newspaper, you may contact the address above. Founded by Dorothy Day and Peter Maurin in 1933, the Catholic Worker Movement is grounded in the firm belief of the God-given dignity of every person. CW communities are committed to nonviolence, voluntary poverty, and hospitality for the homeless, exiled, hungry, and forsaken. Houses are independent of one another and vary in their activities and relationship to the Catholic Church, and in how they incorporate Catholic Worker philosophy and tradition. Most are based on the Gospel, prayer, and Catholic beliefs, but some are interfaith. Catholic Workers live a simple lifestyle in the community, serve the poor, and resist war and social injustice. Most houses need volunteers; contact the house you are interested in directly for further information. The national CW website maintains a complete list of community houses.

Center for Third World Organizing (CTWO)

1218 East 21st Street, Oakland, CA 94606
Tel: (510) 533-7583
Fax: (510) 533-0923
E-mail: training@ctwo.org
Website: www.ctwo.org

CTWO is an organizing and training center that tackles issues affecting third world communities throughout the United States. Community Action Training (CAT) is conducted in the spring, prior to the eight-week Minority Activists Apprenticeship Program (MAAP). MAAP provides training and field experience in techniques of community organizing for young people of color (primarily college students) who are working for social justice. Volunteers receive housing and a stipend. Other internships are sometimes available, including research and writing for partnership programs.

Citizen Action of New York

94 Central Avenue, Albany, NY 12206
Tel: (518) 465-4600, ext. 115
Fax: (518) 465-2890
E-mail: mail@citizenactionny.org or kcasale@citizenactionny.org
Website: www.citizenactionny.org
Contact: Kizzi Casale

Citizen Action of New York (a state affiliate of US Action) works at the grassroots level for racial, social, economic, and environmental justice across New York State. Volunteers work on one of the four current issue campaigns (Education, After-School, Health Care, or Clean Money/Clean Elections) in one of the five state offices, located in Buffalo, Binghamton, Long Island, Brooklyn, and Albany. Volunteers usually work with Citizen Action for a semester or a summer and are required to have some knowledge of American government. Interns and volunteers are expected to pay all living and transportation expenses. Paid internship opportunities occasionally arise based on foundation or grant support and are posted regularly on the website. Contact the communications associate at *nmerrill@citizenactionny.org* or at the phone number above.

Council for Responsible Genetics (CRG)
5 Upland Drive, Suite 3, Cambridge, MA 02140
Tel: (617) 868-0870
Fax: (617) 491-5344
E-mail: crg@gene-watch.org
Website: www.gene-watch.org

CRG is a nonprofit organization fostering public debate about the social, ethical, and environmental implications of genetic technologies. CRG works through the media and concerned citizens to distribute accurate information and represent the public interest on emerging issues in biotechnology. Primary program areas include genetic privacy and discrimination, biological warfare, genetically modified foods, human genetic modification, and reproductive technologies.

Four core principles drive the organization's work:

1. The public must have access to clear and understandable information on technological innovations.

2. The public must be able to participate in public and private decision-making concerning technological developments and their implementation.

3. New technologies must meet social needs.

4. Problems rooted in poverty, racism, and other forms of inequality cannot be remedied by technology alone.

Unpaid internships are available during the summer and during the academic year. Interns should be qualified undergraduate and graduate students interested in bioethics and emerging biotechnologies. Opportunities include working with senior staff and board members on individual research, writing, or outreach projects in specific program areas. Interns should submit application materials to Sujatha Byravan.

Episcopal Urban Internship Program (EUIP) $ ⊞

260 North Locust Street, Inglewood, CA 90301
Tel: (310) 674-7700
Fax: (310) 674-7181
E-mail: euip@euip.org
Website: www.euip.org

EUIP is a one-year voluntary service program for young adults
(from ages 21 to 30). Interns are placed with urban social service
organizations within the Los Angeles area and live communally
in a house in Inglewood. In addition to their job placements,
interns are expected to engage actively in their household community, in spiritual activities, and in the life of the sponsoring
Episcopal parish. Individuals do not need to be Episcopalians
to be urban interns. EUIP provides a monthly stipend, health
insurance, housing, and a car for use in the program. Participants are eligible for an AmeriCorps grant upon completion of
the year. Additional benefits include quarterly retreats and
weekly theological reflection times.

Food First/Institute for Food and Development Policy

(See description of Food First at the back of this book)

The Food Project

555 Dudley Street, Dorchester, MA 02125
Tel: (617) 442-1322
Fax: (617) 442-7918
E-mail: mozeki@thefoodproject.org
Website: www.thefoodproject.org
Contact: Mieko Ozeki, Public Education Associate

The Food Project's mission is to create a thoughtful and productive community of youth and adults from diverse backgrounds working together to build a sustainable food system.
The Food Project's farms in Boston and Lincoln produce
healthy food for residents of the city and its suburbs, provide
youth leadership opportunities, and inspire and support others

to create change in their own communities. Volunteers help on both farms from April through June and from late August through mid-November. They learn about sustainable agricultural practices and food-system as well as food-security issues. Volunteers work from one to three days per week through the growing season. No previous farming experience is required. Volunteers must be at least 15 years of age and those under 18 must have parental consent to work. Occasionally there are volunteer opportunities in the kitchen or with other programs.

InterConnection

124 North 35th Street, Seattle, WA 98103
Tel/Fax: (206) 310-4547
E-mail: brennick@interconnection.org
Website: www.interconnection.org
Contact: Charles Brennick

InterConnection provides nonprofits and NGOs in developing countries with websites, computer and Internet training, and refurbished computers. Though the work may take a volunteer virtually to a country in South and Central America or Africa, because volunteers don't leave home, there aren't any accessibility issues. The only requirement is that volunteers be computer skilled and web savvy. The average time commitment for a placement is one month. Volunteers will incur no costs. Visit the website for more information.

Lutheran Volunteer Corps (LVC)

1226 Vermont Avenue NW, Washington, DC 20005
Tel: (202) 387-3222
Fax: (202) 667-0037
E-mail: lvcrecruitment@lvchome.org
Website: www.lvchome.org

LVC volunteers work in advocacy and public policy, AIDS/HIV, community development and organizing, education, the environment, food and hunger, health care, housing, immigration and refugee services, legal assistance, social and direct services, shelters, and programs for women and youth. Placements are in Baltimore MD, Wilmington DE, Washington DC, Chicago IL, Milwaukee WI, Minneapolis/St. Paul MN, Seattle and Tacoma WA, and Oakland/Berkeley CA. Volunteers live communally with three to six other volunteers, commit to a simplified lifestyle, and work for social justice. Travel, room and board, medical coverage, and daily work-related transportation expenses are covered. The program is open to people of all faiths and ages. Married couples and couples in committed partnerships are welcome to apply. LVC is a Reconciling in Christ Organization. Contact the Recruitment Coordinator.

Mennonite Voluntary Service (MVS)

Mennonite Mission Network
500 South Main Street, PO Box 370, Elkhart, IN 46515
E-mail: info@MennoniteMission.net
Website: www.service.MennoniteMission.net

MVS helps meet the needs of poor and disadvantaged people in the US and Canada. Volunteer placements range from staffing food banks and emergency assistance centers to working with after-school programs. Social work, community organization, housing rehabilitation, and education skills are in particular demand. Initial terms of two years are strongly encouraged, though some assignments are also available for one year. Spanish is helpful or required for some positions. Volunteers must be Christian, at least 20 years old, and from the US or Canada. All expenses are covered by MVS.

National Coalition for the Homeless (NCH)

1012 14th Street NW, Suite 600, Washington, DC 20005-3471
Tel: (202) 737-6444, ext. 19
Fax: (202) 737-6445
E-mail: mstoops@nationalhomeless.org
Website: www.nationalhomeless.org
Contact: Michael Stoops, Director of Community Organizing

NCH works to create the systematic and attitudinal changes necessary to prevent and end homelessness through grassroots organizing, public education, policy advocacy, and technical assistance. NCH also works to meet the immediate needs of those who are homeless or at risk of becoming homeless. Its first principle of practice is getting those who have experienced homelessness involved in all aspects of the organization's work.

Each year NCH offers a limited number of volunteer/internship opportunities. Generally interns are assigned to one of the issue areas of NCH's work: civil rights, health, affordable housing, income, media/publications, or grassroots organizing. Internships last from three weeks to a year. Many of NCH's interns are currently undergraduate or graduate students or have recently graduated. However, others are encouraged to apply. Though interns are expected to pay for their own expenses, students should check with their universities about the possibility of receiving school credit or a stipend. Other NCH internships include a speaker's bureau coordinator and a development coordinator under the auspices of the Ameri-Corps VISTA program, through which interns serve for one year and receive a stipend.

Pesticide Action Network North America (PANNA)

49 Powell Street, Suite 500, San Francisco, CA 94102
Tel: (415) 981-1771
Fax: (415) 981-1991
E-mail: leticia@panna.org
Website: www.panna.org
Contact: Leticia Tirrez, Office Manager

PANNA works to replace pesticide use with ecologically sound and socially just alternatives. As one of five Pesticide Action Network regional centers worldwide, the San Francisco office links local and international consumer, labor, health, environment, and agriculture groups into an international citizens' action network. This network challenges the global proliferation of pesticides, defends basic rights to health and environmental quality, and works to ensure the transition to a just and viable society. PANNA accepts volunteers on a year-round basis. Projects and length of time vary depending on the program's needs. Visit the website for a current list of projects.

Service Civil International
(See listing under International Voluntary Service Organizations)

South Dakota General Convention of Sioux YMCAs
PO Box 218, Dupree, SD 57623
Tel: (605) 365-5232
Fax: (605) 365-5230
E-mail: crandall@siouxymca.org
Website: www.siouxymca.org
Contact: Claudia Wieland-Randall, Executive Director

The Sioux YMCAs are the only ones in the US on Indian reservations. The location on the Cheyenne River Sioux Reservation mostly serves Lakota Sioux families. They offer two types of volunteer opportunities for college-aged or older participants. Volunteers may serve for two months during the summer as staff at YMCA Camp Leslie Marrowbone, working with children 7 to 14 years in age. They also need community development volunteers to live in Dupree while supporting various youth and family programs. These placements last 3 to 12 months. Volunteers must have camp or community work skills, and be flexible and open to a new culture. Both positions provide housing and a stipend.

United Farm Workers of America (UFW)
PO Box 62, Keene, CA 93531
Tel: (661) 823-6250
Fax: (661) 823-6177
E-mail: fwmrecruiter@hotmail.com
Website: www.ufw.org

UFW works for justice for farm workers and safe food for consumers. They are now conducting the largest agricultural worker organizing campaign in over 20 years. UFW is seeking talented and motivated organizers to be part of this groundbreaking campaign in California. Prospective candidates must be able to speak Spanish, and we prefer those who have bilingual writing abilities. UFW offers competitive salaries and benefits, depending on an applicant's prior experience.

Volunteer Missionary Movement (VMM)
(See listing under International Voluntary Service Organizations)

6

Alternative Travel and Study Overseas

I N THIS SECTION YOU WILL FIND SHORTER-TERM VOLUN-
teer opportunities as well as options for travel to unusual destinations. A brief work stint with one of the organizations listed
here (say a two-week excursion building a well in Nicaragua
with El Porvenir) can acquaint you with living in poor countries and help you decide if a long-term commitment makes
sense for you. A number of groups conduct "reality tours," study
tours, or delegations in developing countries and the US. These
are socially responsible educational tours that provide participants with firsthand experience of the political, economic, and
social structures that create or sustain hunger, poverty, and
environmental degradation. Tour participants meet with people from diverse sectors with various perspectives on issues of
agriculture, development, and the environment. They often stay
with local people, visit rural areas, and meet with grassroots
organizers. The experience and insights gained on such a tour
may influence participants' future work for democratic social
change. Many universities offer study-abroad programs. This
section mentions just a few of these.

Amizade, Ltd.
(See listing under International Voluntary Service Organizations)

Bike-Aid

Global Exchange
2017 Mission Street, Suite 303, San Francisco, CA 94110
Tel: (415) 255-7296 or (800) RIDE-808
E-mail: bikeaid@globalexchange.org
Website: globalexchange.org

Bike-Aid is an innovative cross-country cycling adventure sponsored by Global Exchange. Global Exchange is a nonprofit human rights organization working for global political, economic, environmental, and social justice. Bike-Aid combines physical challenge, community interaction, global education, leadership, fund-raising, and service learning into the empowering experience of a lifetime. Every summer individuals from around the world cycle across the country (starting in San Francisco or Seattle to Washington DC) or take a two-week California coastal ride to the Mexican border. There is a new ride in December in which cyclists journey through the Hawaiian Islands. Along the routes, participants exchange information and get a firsthand look into local community groups, the issues that are facing them, and the solutions that are taking place. Overnight lodging includes organic farms, Native American Indian reservations or indigenous communities, churches, and camping in some of the most beautiful spots the US has to offer.

Beginners to prize-winning racers have participated in Bike-Aid, and riders from the ages of 16 to 60 have met the challenge. It is not a race, and Global Exchange encourages the participation of people from all backgrounds, ages, and abilities. Cyclists must be willing to live in a community throughout the summer, and intern/volunteers must be resourceful and able to work in a team environment.

Center for Global Education
Augsburg College
2211 Riverside Avenue, Minneapolis, MN 55454
Tel: (800) 299-8889 or (612) 330-1159
Fax: (612) 330-1695
E-mail: globaled@augsburg.edu
Website: www.centerforglobaleducation.org

The Center for Global Education designs and coordinates travel seminars to Central America, Mexico, the Caribbean, and Southern Africa. The goal is to foster critical analysis of local and global conditions so that personal and systemic change takes place. Participants meet with a wide range of representatives in government and business, church, and grassroots communities. Their focus is on sustainable development, human rights, women's roles, and the role and responsibility of people in working for social change. The center's programs are utilized by a wide variety of civic groups, churches, colleges, and individuals. They also arrange longer study programs for undergraduate students.

Christian Peacemaker Teams (CPT)
PO Box 6508, Chicago, IL 60680-6508
Tel: (773) 277-0253
Fax: (773) 277-0291
E-mail: peacemakers@cpt.org
Website: www.cpt.org

CPT leads short-term study delegations several times yearly to areas of conflict and/or heightened militarization. CPT is cross-denominational with strong roots grounded in the Quakers, Mennonites, and Church of the Brethren. Study tour participants are self-funded and should be at least 18 years of age.

(Also listed under International Voluntary Service Organizations)

Christians for Peace in El Salvador (CRISPAZ)

122 DeWitt Drive, Boston, MA 02120
Tel: (617) 445-5115
Fax: (617) 249-0769
Email: info@crispaz.org
Website: www.crispaz.org

Founded in 1984, CRISPAZ is a faith-based organization dedicated to mutual accompaniment with the church of the poor
and marginalized communities in El Salvador. In building
bridges of solidarity between communities in El Salvador and
those in their home countries, CRISPAZ volunteers strive
together for peace, justice, and human liberation. El Salvador
Encounter is a faith-based experience in which participants
can learn about current Salvadoran reality. Encounters are
seven to ten days long and offer the opportunity to explore a
different reality and build relationships with people of a different culture.

(Also listed under International Voluntary Service Organizations)

Co-op America Travel-Links

120 Beacon Street, Somerville, MA 02143
Tel: (800) 648-2667
Fax: (617) 492-3720
E-mail: mj@tvlcoll.com

Travel-Links is a full-service travel agency that emphasizes
responsible tourism and seeks to promote understanding and
cooperation among people through nonexploitative travel.
Make your travel dollars count.

Cultural Restoration Tourism Project (CRTP)

410 Paloma Avenue, Pacifica, CA 94044
Tel: (415) 563-7221
E-mail: info@crtp.net
Website: www.crtp.net

With its focus on restoring Buddhist temples, CRTP is currently sponsoring a new project in Nepal that is similar to the ongoing one in Mongolia. In Mongolia in the summer of 1999, CRTP began the restoration of the Baldan Baraivan temple, built in the 1700s, badly damaged in the 1930s by the Soviet regime, and one of the few standing Buddhist monasteries of its kind. CRTP is funding and executing the restoration of the main temple. Tours are available to the general public each summer through the project's completion, currently scheduled for 2006. Participants do not need any construction experience, just a will and a desire to see the temple rebuilt. Local community members are employed full time and participants work alongside Mongolian staff. Everyone stays in traditional yurts, each of which houses from two to three people. Opportunities for overnights in the wilderness are available; travelers should bring their own tents if interested in camping or desiring private accommodations. For both the Mongolia and Nepal restoration projects CRTP uses a "volunteer vacation" model that entails a participant donation of approximately $150 per day. For the most current project information, check the website.

Earthwatch Institute

3 Clock Tower Place, Maynard, MA 01754-0075
Tel: (800) 776-0188 or (978) 461-0081
E-mail: info@earthwatch.org
Website: www.earthwatch.org

Earthwatch sponsors scholarly field research worldwide and enables volunteers to assist scientists on their various expeditions. Most of the projects study endangered ecosystems, biodiversity, and resource management, but a handful each year center on public health and sustainable development. For example, volunteers in 2005 may work with the Nalamdana project, directed by Nithya Balaji, using street theater to teach public health and nutrition to mothers in Tamil Nadu, southern India. Other volunteers may work with communities in the Samburu-Laikipia region of Kenya to develop ways of helping local pastoral people coexist with wildlife, given increasing competition for water and land resources. Or, volunteers may work with Dr. Alain Touwaide of the Smithsonian, who is studying Renaissance texts to discover the medicinal plants used by the ancient Romans. Project teams last from one to two weeks and no special skills are required—all are welcome. Project contributions range from $700 to $3,000 and do not include airfare to the research site.

Explorations in Travel, Inc.
2458 River Road, Guilford, VT 05301
Tel: (802) 257-0152
Fax: (802) 257-2784
E-mail: explore@volunteertravel.com
Website: www.volunteertravel.com or www.exploretravel.com

Explorations in Travel provides individual volunteer work placements for students and adults from all over the world. Placements can be arranged in Belize, Costa Rica, Ecuador, Guatemala, and Puerto Rico. Work sites include schools, wildlife rehabilitation centers, animal shelters, and sustainable ecotourism projects. Language classes can be incorporated into a placement. Fees are $975; there is a nonrefundable application fee of $35. Both individual and group programs are available. Explorations in Travel can also help with flight arrangements and fund-raising ideas.

Fourth World Movement/USA
(See listing under International Voluntary Service Organizations)

Global Citizens Network (GCN)
130 North Howell Street, St. Paul, MN 55104
Tel: (800) 644-9292 or (651) 644-0960
E-mail: info@globalcitizens.org
Website: www.globalcitizens.org

GCN offers individuals the opportunity to interact with people of diverse cultures in order to develop creative and effective local solutions to global problems. GCN sends short-term teams of volunteers to communities in other countries. Each team is partnered with a grassroots organization active in meeting community needs. Volunteers assist and work under the direction of local people on locally initiated projects, staying with host families or living as a group at a community center. Each team member receives training materials and participates in an orientation session. Groups are led by GCN team leaders. Tours last one to three weeks, including travel time. Participant expenses run from $650 to $1,950, excluding airfare. This covers most medical and evacuation insurance, training materials, a donation to the project, and a portion of our program costs. Children ages 8 to 12 are half price; returning former volunteers receive a discount as well. Expenses are tax deductible in the United States. There are no upper age restrictions; volunteers ages 8 to 17 must be accompanied by a parent or guardian. No specific skills are required. Project work ranges from school or road repair to water and sanitation projects to trail renovation. Current sites include Guatemala, Kenya, Mexico, Nepal, Tanzania, and Native American reservations in Arizona, New Mexico, and Washington.

Global Exchange (GX)

2017 Mission Street, Suite 303, San Francisco, CA 94110
Tel: (415) 255-7296
Fax: (415) 255-7498
E-mail: realitytours@globalexchange.org
Website: www.globalexchange.org

GX organizes reality tours, study seminars, and human rights delegations to more than 25 countries. These study tours offer a unique opportunity to learn firsthand about pressing issues confronting the third world. Tour participants meet with peasant and labor organizers, community and religious leaders, peace activists, environmentalists, scholars, students, indigenous leaders, and government officials. Countries visited include South Africa, Zimbabwe, Cuba, Haiti, Israel/Palestine, Iran, Mexico (Chiapas and the US-Mexico border), Central America, Vietnam, Northern Ireland, Ecuador, Brazil, and Afghanistan. Costs range from $800 to $3,200. Our delegations provide an educational introduction to a country that often leads participants to develop connections with organizations where they can volunteer. The breadth of our international connections to grassroots level organizers is the GX advantage.

Green Belt Safaris

Bridges to Community
95 Croton Avenue, Ossining, NY 10562
Tel: (914) 923-2200
E-mail: info@bridgestocommunity.org
Website: www. bridgestocommunity.org

The Green Belt Safari is a two-week trip to Kenya organized by Bridges to Community and facilitated by the Green Belt Movement (GBM)—one of East Africa's foremost environmental organizations founded by Nobel Peace Prize winner Wangari Maathai. For part of the trip, participants stay at the GBM Nairobi headquarters, learning about its work and about Kenyan culture and politics. They also travel to rural Kenya, staying with families in a village and assisting with the movement's ongoing conservations work. The trip includes a visit to one of Kenya's wildlife centers to examine the relationship between animal conservation and rural community development, and a visit to archaeological sites in the Rift Valley to explore their implications for a new creation story. Throughout the tour participants examine problems and concerns between north and south in a postcolonial world marked by interdependent global markets. Cost of the 14-day journey is $1,750 for students and $2,250 for adults, plus airfare. Family group discounts and limited partial scholarships are available. The fee includes accommodations, meals, internal travel, and a contribution to GBM. Contact by phone or e-mail for further information and reservations.

Heifer International

Attn: Study Tour Coordinator
1015 Louisiana Street, Little Rock, AR 72202
Tel: (800) 422-0474
E-mail: studytours@heifer.org
Website: www.heifer.org

Heifer International is a worldwide community development organization that provides farm animals, as well as training and related agricultural and community-building services, to farmers in developing areas in 49 countries, including 23 states in the US. Heifer conducts 8- to 20-day study tours to its program areas. Groups meet Heifer in-country staff and learn about sustainable development. Through visits to Heifer project partners, participants hear people's stories. Heifer study tours —rather than being work trips—foster information gathering and critical thinking, so that participants return motivated to take action toward the Heifer vision: "A world of communities living together in peace and equitably sharing the resources of a healthy planet." Heifer trips range in cost from $2,000 to $5,500, and usually include international airfare (where applicable). For more information, go to the website and look for "Get Involved" and "Study Tours."

Ibike/Bicycle Africa
International Bicycle Fund (IBF)

4887 Columbia Drive South, Suite Q, Seattle, WA 98108-1919
Tel/Fax: (206) 767-0848
E-mail: ibike@ibike.org
Website: www.ibike.org/bikeafrica/index.htm or for all other programs
    www.ibike.org

IBF arranges from two- to four-week cultural immersion, educational bicycle tours in these African nations: Benin, Cameroon, Eritrea, Ethiopia, Gambia, Ghana, Kenya, Malawi, Mali, Senegal, South Africa, Tanzania, Togo, Tunisia, Uganda, and Zimbabwe. Other similarly assembled programs visit Cuba, Ecuador, Guyana, Korea, Nepal, the US, and Vietnam. Area specialists accompany each program. Cycling is moderate and participants do not need to have extensive touring experience. Costs range from $900 to $2,500, not including airfare. IBF promotes bicycle transportation, economic development, international understanding, and safety education.

Institute for Central American Development Studies (ICADS)

Dept. 826, PO Box 025216, Miami, FL 33102-5216
E-mail: info@icads.org or info@icadscr.com
Website: www.icads.org or www.icadscr.com
In Costa Rica: Apdo. 300-2050, San Pedro Montes de Oca, San Jose,
    Costa Rica
Tel: 011 (506) 225-0508
Fax: 011 (506) 234-1337

A teaching center for Central American social and environmental issues, ICADS offers four separate and unique study programs in Costa Rica and Nicaragua:

1. The Intensive Spanish Immersion Program is a four-week language program with classes of four and a half hours, five days per week. Small classes (four students or less) are geared to individual needs. Lectures and cultural/community-service activities focus on environmental issues, women's studies, economic development, education, and health care. Programs begin the first Monday of each month and cost $1,700.

2. The 14-week Semester Internship Program includes one-month course work in Central American social justice issues together with intensive Spanish and a two-month structured internship in Costa Rica or Nicaragua. Internships may focus on women's studies or issues of environment/ecology, health care, education, community development, etc. During fall or spring terms, students earn 15 semester credits. Tuition is $8,500.

3. The Summer Internship Program is a ten-week, not-for-credit version of the previous program for undergrads,

graduates, and professionals. Running from June through August, program tuition is $3,800.

4. The 14-week Field Course in Resource Management and Sustainable Development is an interdisciplinary semester-length program looking at development from ecological and socioeconomic perspectives. It includes four weeks of intensive Spanish and study of urban issues (e.g., waste management, housing, structural adjustment, assembly industry); five weeks in different managed and natural ecosystems learning techniques of social science field research (e.g., banana transnationals, agriculture, community cooperatives, cloud forest and watershed management); and five weeks of independent study where volunteers live in rural or urban communities. During the fall or spring terms, students earn 15 semester credits. Tuition is $8,500.

Susan Smith, Spanish Program, ICADS

Across the street from the US Embassy is the neighborhood of Pavas, a slum of tin houses built on a mountain of trash. We crossed the creek on rotten planks and stared at the disgusting water. The smell was wretched and the sights saddening. Trash was organized and packed down to make stairs. We carried pieces of wood through the maze of broken homes and human filth. We are helping an organization whose objective is to give every child a bed.

We entered the people's houses and our mouths dropped at the lumpy dirt floors, the tin roofs with holes, and the "toilets" (only pots) in corners. People made big barrels into ovens. Naked children stared at us. Old people hid behind "windows" (cracks in walls). We built five beds in two hours in the oven-baking houses. Our feet fell through huge holes in "floors" (boards crossed together like puzzles). The hair in our noses curled from the stench. Now ten children can sleep off the floor.

International Partnership for Service-Learning and Leadership (IPSL)

815 2nd Avenue, Suite 315, New York, NY 10017
Tel: (212) 986-0989
Fax: (212) 986-5039
E-mail: info@ipsl.org
Website: www.ipsl.org

IPSL offers programs that integrate volunteer community service and formal academic study abroad for credit. Programs
are available in the Czech Republic, Ecuador (Galapagos,
Guayaquil, and Quito), England, France, India, Israel, Jamaica,
Mexico, the Philippines, Russia, Scotland, Thailand, and the US
(with Native Americans in South Dakota). Each location offers
a variety of community service projects such as basic education, aid to the handicapped, women's issues, recreation, social
welfare, and health. Costs range from $3,700 to $11,200 per
term. Participants are primarily undergraduate students for
summer, fall/spring, full-year, or January and August interses-
sions. IPSL also offers a one-year master's degree in International Service in Jamaica or Mexico (first semester) and the
United Kingdom (second semester and thesis).

Interreligious Foundation for Community Organization (IFCO)
Pastors for Peace

402 West 145th Street, New York, NY 10031
Tel: (212) 926-5757
Fax: (212) 926-5842
E-mail: ifco@igc.org
Website: www.ifconews.org

Pastors for Peace is an action/education project of IFCO and
includes activists from all sectors of society. Pastors for Peace
organizes humanitarian aid caravans, work brigades, delegations, and study tours to Cuba, Central America, and Mexico.
Churches, schools, and other organizations can name the dates

and help define the itinerary of customized study tours and construction brigades for their members. Call Pastors for Peace for more information and applications.

Los Niños
(See listing under International Voluntary Service Organizations)

Marazul Charters, Inc.
725 River Road, Edgewater, NJ 07020
Tel: (800) 223-5334 or (201) 840-6711
Fax: (201) 840-6719
E-mail: info@marazul.com or (for Venezuela trips)
    venezuela@marazul.com
Website: www.marazul.com

Since 1979 Marazul has sent more than 300,000 people to Cuba. As a fully licensed travel service provider, Marazul assists licensed individuals and educational, religious, and humanitarian groups with all aspects of travel including air arrangements to Cuba on direct flights from Miami, as well as flights through third countries such as Canada, Mexico, the Bahamas, and Jamaica; Cuban visas; and land arrangements from accommodations and transportation to meetings, visits, and exchanges. Special charters can be arranged for individual groups or organizations. In 2005 Marazul begins new programs to Venezuela (see the country specific e-mail address above). Bilingual in Spanish and English and a member of the American Society of Travel Agents, Marazul is a fully computerized, full-service travel agency that is ready to reserve your flights and hotels throughout the world.

Mexico Solidarity Network (MSN)
4834 North Springfield, Chicago, IL 60625
Tel: (773) 583-7728
Fax: (773) 583-7738
E-mail: msn@mexicosolidarity.org
Website: www.mexicosolidarity.org

MSN is a network of US grassroots organizations supporting economic and social justice and democracy on both sides of the US-Mexico border. Their focus is on globalization and neo-liberal economic policies that affect border communities as well as the indigenous population of Chiapas. MSN also sponsors US speaking tours for Mexican activists and educational delegations to Mexico.

Middle East Children's Alliance (MECA)

901 Parker Street, Berkeley, CA 94710
Tel: (510) 548-0542
Fax: (510) 548-0543
E-mail: meca@mecaforpeace.org
Website: www.mecaforpeace.org

MECA raises funds for humanitarian aid (medical supplies, school books, food, and clothing) for children in Iraq, the West Bank, and Gaza. For 16 years MECA has taken North Americans into Israel and the Occupied Palestinian Territories (OPT) to see for themselves the effects of over 50 years of apartheid and occupation.

Over the course of a 14-day trip participants cover a lot of political and geographical territory. The MECA aim is to provide delegates with information about the current political situation as well as insights into the daily lives of people living under occupation and within the specter of Israeli apartheid. Their hosts are activists, academics, health-care workers, refugees, and international aid workers. By bearing witness, participants come away with a stronger understanding of the issues facing Palestinians in the OPT and Israel. On their return, participants are well prepared to help others understand these issues.

(Also listed under International Voluntary Service Organizations)

Minnesota Studies in International Development (MSID)

University of Minnesota, Learning Abroad Center, 230 Heller Hall,
   271 19th Avenue South, Minneapolis, MN 55455-0340
Tel: (612) 626-9000
Fax: (612) 626-8009
E-mail: UMabroad@umn.edu
Website: www.UMabroad.umn.edu

MSID is a credit-bearing study abroad program that combines intensive classroom work with individualized internships and research opportunities in grassroots development and social change projects in rural and urban settings alike. MSID offers programs in Ecuador, Ghana, India, Kenya, and Senegal, with three enrollment options at each site: academic year, fall semester, and spring semester. Juniors, seniors, college graduates, and graduate students are eligible to apply. Tuition and fees vary from site to site. Students with disabilities can often be accommodated.

Mobility International USA (MIUSA)

PO Box 10767, Eugene, OR 97440 or 45 West Broadway, Suite 202,
   Eugene, OR 97401
Tel: (541) 343-1284 (voice/TTY)
Fax: (541) 343-6812
E-mail: info@miusa.org
Website: www.miusa.org

MIUSA's international exchanges specialize in leadership training, community service, cross-cultural experiential learning, and advocacy for the rights and inclusion of people with disabilities. These short-term group exchanges for youth, adults, and professionals with and without disabilities take place in the United States and abroad. MIUSA has coordinated exchanges with Azerbaijan, Bulgaria, China, Costa Rica, East Asia, Germany, Italy, Japan, Mexico, Russia, the United Kingdom, and other countries. Activities include training seminars and workshops, adaptive recreational activities, cross-cultural communication, language classes, and volunteer service projects. Exchanges vary from ten days to three weeks in length.

MIUSA's National Clearinghouse on Disability and Exchange (NCDE) provides additional information on international exchange, volunteer, and community service opportunities. NCDE staff can respond to inquiries on the range of opportunities available and on how people with disabilities can make these possibilities a reality.

Nicaragua Network
(See listing under International Voluntary Service Organizations)

our developing world (odw)
13004 Paseo Presada, Saratoga, CA 95070-4125
Tel: (408) 379-4431
Fax: (408) 376-0755
E-mail: odw@magiclink.net
Website: www.magiclink.net/~odw

The main focus of odw is to bring the realities of the third world and the richness of diverse cultures to North Americans through programs in schools, churches, and community groups. Once a year odw takes a small group of travelers who want a firsthand experience on a reality tour. Past destinations have included Cambodia, Cuba, Guatemala, Honduras, Laos, Mozambique, Nicaragua, the Philippines, South Africa, Vietnam, Zimbabwe, and Indigenous Hawaii. odw expects to tour South Africa in 2005, Central America and/or the Caribbean in 2006, and Southeast Asia (Cambodia, Laos, and Vietnam) in 2007. By providing an opportunity to talk with peasants, workers, women's associations, health workers, and co-op members, odw tours give participants a chance to learn about health, agrarian reform, human rights and educational campaigns, and economic and social planning.

Plowshares Institute

PO Box 243, Simsbury, CT 06070
Tel: (860) 651-4304
Fax: (860) 651-4305
E-mail: plowshares@plowsharesinstitute.org
Website: www.plowsharesinstitute.org

Plowshares traveling seminars initiate cross-cultural dialogue between peoples of developed and developing nations. Participants commit both to intensive preparation before departure and community education upon return. Trip itineraries include meetings with religious and civic leaders, home stay experiences, and visits to development projects. The Institute plans two-week programs to several countries including Brazil, China, Cuba, Indonesia, Uganda, and South Africa. Check the website for more information.

El Porvenir

2508 42nd Street, Sacramento, CA 95817
Tel: (303) 520-0093
Fax: (916) 227-5068
E-mail: jemerritt@elporvenir.org
Website: www.elporvenir.org

El Porvenir supports self-help sustainable development in poor rural communities in Nicaragua through funding and technical aid to community-requested water, sanitation, and reforestation projects. El Porvenir sponsors one- to two-week work trips and one-week educational tours to Nicaragua eight times per year. The cost of the educational tour is $1,200 per person, plus airfare to Nicaragua; the cost of the work trip is $950 for two weeks or $800 for one week, plus airfare. Work trip participants stay in modest hostels and work alongside community members to construct a project. Educational tours visit various El Porvenir project villages and engage in cultural and recreational activities. No Spanish or construction experience is required. Work groups are limited to ten people. All groups are accompanied at all times by bilingual El Porvenir staff.

School for International Training (SIT)
SIT TESOL Certificate Program

Kipling Road, PO Box 676, Brattleboro, VT 05302–0676
Tel: (802) 258–3310
Fax: (802) 258–3316
E-mail: tesolcert@sit.edu
Website: www.sit.edu/tesolcert/

The SIT TESOL Certificate Program is a 130-hour, intensive four-week course providing practical teacher training through demonstrations, lesson planning and analysis, practice teaching, and feedback. In some locations, practitioners may choose to study more extensively over a longer period. Certification sites include Australia, Brazil, Costa Rica, Japan, Poland, Spain, Thailand, and the US. Visit the website for more information.

(See listing under Resources)

Third World Opportunities Program (TWO)

779 Fulton Road, San Marcos, CA 92069
Tel: (760) 471–8240
E-mail: severinelaine@aol.com

TWO is a hunger- and poverty-awareness program that fosters an appropriate response to human need. It seeks to encourage sensitivity to life in the third world, intentional reflection on our relationship with third world people, effective work projects that offer practical services to the hungry, homeless, and poor, and organized efforts to change existing conditions. Offering a double-focus program, TWO consists of an awareness tour along the US-Mexico border followed by a short-term work project such as a six-day service assignment at orphanages in Tecate and Las Palmas, Mexico. Participant cost is $250 for the six-day journey from San Diego, which includes meals, accommodations, administration, building materials, and support of the orphanage (but not does not include transportation).

Ufufuo, Inc. $ ▓

1225 Geranium Street NW, Washington, DC 20012
Tel: (202) 722-1461
Fax: (202) 723-5376
E-mail: hjconfer@worldnet.att.net
Website: http://ufufuo.home.att.net
Contact: Harold Confer, Director

Ufufuo, Inc. is a public charity that grew out of the church-
rebuilding movement of the 1990s. Their interfaith, international volunteers rebuild damaged or destroyed churches,
mosques, or synagogues in the US and overseas. In 2004 they
rebuilt a damaged church in Kenya. When congregations find
rebuilding resources and request Ufufuo's assistance working
under their contractor, Ufufuo plans new projects. Domestic
volunteers commit to a minimum of one week and international volunteers commit to a minimum of one month. After
paying the nonrefundable $25 application fee, the participant
cost for domestic work camps is $165 per week. International
work camp volunteers cover their own passport, visa, inocula-
tion, and discretionary spending costs, but scholarships cover
on-site costs. All volunteers are required to have health insurance and provide their own transportation to and from projects. Interested persons ages 17 and older should review the
website for upcoming project information and downloadable
application forms.

US Servas

11 John Street, Suite 505, New York, NY 10038
Tel: (212) 267-0252
Fax: (212) 267-0292
E-mail: info@usservas.org
Website: www.usservas.org

US Servas fosters a more just and peaceful world by promoting
appreciation of cultural differences through home stays and
experiences in volunteered host communities. During short-

term (two-night) stays, travelers share aspects of their home and community life while discussing concerns about social and international problems. Some hosts offer longer visits. The application consists of an interview, two character references, and an $85 membership fee. Send a SASE to receive an application or download one from the website.

Venceremos Brigade

PO Box 5202, Englewood, NJ 07631–05202
Tel: (212) 560-4360
E-mail: vbrigade@yahoo.com
Website: www.vbrigade.org

During Venceremos Brigade participants' two-week travel to Cuba, they visit schools, factories, clinics, and hospitals; have informal visits and discussions with Cubans; and participate in educational seminars with representatives from other countries. Brigade members also engage in work camp activities. Each participant must be at least 18 years old, a US citizen with a valid passport, and not currently in military service. Upon acceptance, participants attend a series of preparatory sessions; they commit to work on some aspect of Brigade educational projects after returning. Brigade committees are located in various areas throughout the US.

Voices on the Border

Educational Delegations
1600 Webster Street NE, Washington, DC 20017
Tel: (202) 529-2912
Fax: (202) 529-0897
E-mail: voices@votb.org
Website: www.votb.org

Voices on the Border brings together rural communities of former war refugees with concerned groups and individuals in the US. The relationships that form help sustain Salvadoran communities both spiritually and financially, and provide US participants with an essential perspective on a different world. Voices supports community organizing that unites people to fight for their rights, and development projects to help people meet their basic needs and create sustainable sources of income. Voices sponsors several delegations a year to El Salvador to meet these communities and Salvadoran social justice organizations. Where possible, delegates stay with families in the countryside. The 7- to 14-day delegation includes all on-the-ground expenses and costs about $75 per day plus airfare. Contact our national office for more information.

World-Wide Opportunities on Organic Farms Independents (WWOOF)

PO Box 2675, Lewes, East Sussex, BN7 1RB, United Kingdom
Tel/Fax: 011 (44 0) 1273-476-286
E-mail: hello@wwoof.org
Website: www.wwoof.org

WWOOF provides those who would like to volunteer on organic farms with a list of host farms throughout the world. The purpose of WWOOF is to enable people to learn firsthand about organic growing techniques, expose urban dwellers to farm life and work, and help farmers make organic production a viable alternative. WWOOF organizations exist in many countries (e.g. Australia, Germany, Ghana, Italy, New Zealand, Switzerland, the United Kingdom, the United States, etc.), and WWOOF host farms exist even in countries without a WWOOF headquarters. Hosts in France, Ireland, Portugal, South Africa, Spain, and many countries in Latin America are listed with WWOOF Independents. If you would like to volunteer in a specific country, contact that country's WWOOF organization; if there isn't one, contact WWOOF Independents in the United Kingdom, either through the website or by writing and enclosing a SASE and an international reply coupon (available at any post office). A list of national WWOOF organizations can be found on the website.

Farm opportunities vary in the amount of skill or experience expected, but many hosts require none. Room and board are provided at all sites. Volunteers should keep in mind that WWOOF is merely a contact service. It provides the address of the farm, but the volunteer must work out the placement with the host and obtain any necessary visas and work permits.

7

RESOURCES

Other Organizations

These groups do not generally sponsor intern or travel programs; they distribute information about volunteer or travel opportunities, foreign countries, underrepresented cultures, or aspects of development.

Bank Information Center (BIC)
733 15th Street NW, Suite 1126, Washington, DC 20005
Tel: (202) 737-7752
Fax: (202) 737-1155
E-mail: info@bicusa.org
Website: www.bicusa.org
Contact: Leslie Greene, Information Services Coordinator

BIC provides hard-to-obtain information on the projects and policies of multilateral development banks (like the World Bank) to environmental and social justice organizations in developing countries. The Center offers numerous publications and reports and advocates for greater transparency in World Bank operations. There is much documentation here of the processes by which development is managed and mismanaged.

Center for Community Change (CCC)
1000 Wisconsin Avenue NW, Washington, DC 20007
Tel: (202) 342-0519
E-mail: info@communitychange.org
Website: www.communitychange.org

SOUTHERN CALIFORNIA (FIELD) OFFICE:
8201 4th Street, Suite G, Downey, CA 90241
Tel: (562) 862-2070
E-mail: LAOffice@communitychange.org

For more than 30 years, CCC has helped grassroots organizations build their communities' capacity for self-help by training community organizers and providing technical assistance to community organizations. The website contains information on aspects of poverty in the US—including housing, jobs, transportation, health, and policy—and profiles of advocacy projects with which CCC has assisted. The site also includes downloadable reports, the online newsletter CCC News, policy alerts, facts and figures on wealth distribution, and a list of groups besides CCC that train community organizers.

CIVICUS: World Alliance for Citizen Participation
1112 16th Street NW, Suite 540, Washington, DC 20036
Tel: (202) 331-8518
Fax: (202) 331-8774
E-mail: info@civicus.org
Website: www.civicus.org

CIVICUS is an international alliance dedicated to strengthening citizen action and civil society throughout the world, especially in areas where participatory democracy and freedom of citizen association are threatened. The website contains links to its many member NGOs. The organization publishes books and a bimonthly newsletter following trends and offering analyses on the third sector movement worldwide. Its atlas, available free online as well as in other formats, profiles the state of civil society in dozens of countries—size and scope, economic impact, legal and tax framework, state of relations with government and business sectors, and names of resource organizations.

Civil Society International (CSI)
2929 NE Blakeley Street, Seattle, WA 98105
Tel: (206) 523-4755
E-mail: csi@civilsoc.org
Website: www.civilsoc.org
CSI assists independent organizations worldwide working for freedom and civil society in nations unfriendly to these principles. It provides assistance mainly in the form of information, networking, and educational resources.

Council on International Educational Exchange (CIEE)
7 Custom House Street, 3rd Floor, Portland, ME 04101
Tel: (800) 407-8839 or (207) 553-7600
Fax: (207) 553-7699
E-mail: studyinfo@ciee.org
Website: www.ciee.org
CIEE offers a range of study abroad, travel, volunteer, and internship programs for youth, college students, recent graduates, and teachers.

Cultural Survival, Inc.
215 Prospect Street, Cambridge, MA 02139
Tel: (617) 441-5400
Fax: (617) 441-5417
E-mail: culturalsurvival@cs.org
Website: www.cs.org
Cultural Survival, Inc., promotes the cause of self-determination for indigenous peoples worldwide, provides organizational support and fiscal sponsorship for projects in indigenous communities, and publishes reports on a host of topics relating to development.

Focus on the Global South
c/o CUSRI, Chulalongkorn University
Bangkok 10330, Thailand
Tel: 011 (66 2) 218-7363 or 011 (66 2) 218-7364 or 011 (66 2) 218-7365
Fax: 011 (66 2) 255-9976
E-mail: admin@focusweb.org
Website: www.focusweb.org

Focus on the Global South supports a program of progressive development policy research and practice dedicated to regional and global policy analysis and advocacy work. Its emphasis is on the developing nations of the Southern Hemisphere, particularly the Asia-Pacific region. Many of Focus' articles and reports are available online. Focus has accepted several short-term interns and volunteers in the past. Priorities are on applicants from the South, who are self-funding and have skills that match Focus campaign and program needs at the particular time. Due to limited office and staff capacity, usually only one person is accepted at a time.

(Also listed under International Voluntary Service Organizations)

Fund for Reconciliation and Development (FRD)
355 West 39th Street, New York, NY 10018
Tel: (212) 760-9903
Fax: (212) 760-9906
E-mail: info@ffrd.org
Website: www.ffrd.org
FRD promotes cooperation between US nonprofit organizations and their counterparts in Cambodia, Cuba, Laos, and Vietnam. FRD organizes conferences in the United States and publishes a quarterly newsletter, Interchange.

Grassroots International
179 Boylston Street, 4th Floor, Boston, MA 02130
Tel: (617) 524-1400
Fax: (617) 524-5525
E-mail: info@grassrootsonline.org
Website: www.grassrootsonline.org
Through cash grants and material aid, Grassroots International supports the work of NGOs in Brazil, Eritrea, Haiti, Mexico, and Palestine. It also performs education and advocacy on a range of issues.

InterAction: American Council for Voluntary International Action
1717 Massachusetts Avenue NW, Suite 701, Washington, DC 20036
Tel: (202) 667-8227
Fax: (202) 667-8236
E-mail: publications@interaction.org
Website: www.interaction.org

InterAction is the largest alliance of US-based international development and humanitarian nongovernmental organizations. With more than 160 members operating in every developing country, InterAction works to overcome poverty, exclusion, and suffering by advancing social justice and basic dignity for all. Monday Developments, a biweekly newsletter, provides in-depth news and commentary on global trends that affect relief, refugee, and development work, as well as job opportunity listings throughout the world. InterAction also publishes *Member Profiles,* a biannual directory of its members; *Global Work,* a guide for volunteer, internship, and fellowship opportunities in international development abroad; and a weekly e-mail listing of extensive employment and internship opportunities in the international development and assistance field. For subscriptions, job listings, or advertising, please contact Nicole Duciaume at (202) 667-8227, ext. 121, or at *nduciaume@interaction.org.*

International Development Exchange (IDEX)
827 Valencia Street, Suite 101, San Francisco, CA 94110
Tel: (415) 824-8384
E-mail: info@idex.org
Website: www.idex.org

IDEX is a nonprofit organization that partners with grassroots organizations in Africa, Asia, and Latin America while simultaneously informing and engaging North Americans about challenges facing these communities. Since 1985 IDEX has channeled over $2.6 million to fund more than 500 self-help community projects, promoting social change and economic independence for persons earning less than $1 a day—particularly women, youth, and indigenous peoples.

The International Ecotourism Society (TIES)
733 15th Street NW, Suite 1000, Washington, DC 20005
Tel: (202) 347-9203
Fax: (202) 387-7915
E-mail: ecomail@ecotourism.org
Website: www.ecotourism.org

TIES is an international membership organization dedicated to disseminating information about ecologically sound and sustainable tourism. Individual memberships start at $35 per year and include subscription to the TIES newsletter, discounts on TIES publications, and access to lists of tour and lodge operators.

International Volunteer Programs Association (IVPA)
PO Box 18, Presque Isle, MI 49777
Tel: (989) 595-3667
E-mail: international_IVPA@yahoo.com
Website: www.volunteerinternational.org

IVPA is an alliance of nonprofit, nongovernmental organizations based in the Americas that are involved in international volunteer and internship exchanges. IVPA's website has a database of volunteer opportunities as well as general advice on fund-raising and traveling abroad.

Panos Institute (PI)
1322 18th Street NW, Suite 26, Washington, DC 20036
Tel: (202) 429-0730
E-mail: panosinstitute@earthlink.net
Website: www.panosinst.org

PI specializes in news and research about development issues, and aims to stimulate public debate by providing accessible information on neglected or poorly understood topics as they affect the developing world, particularly in the fields of poverty, gender, environment, reproductive health, and population. PI publishes books, feature articles, briefings, and collected oral testimonies.

SANGONet

PO Box 31392, Braamfontein, South Africa 2017
Tel: 011 (27 11) 403-4935
Fax: 011 (27 11) 403-0130
E-mail: (through website)
Website: www.sangonet.org.za

Over the last 17 years, South Africa's nonprofit Internet service provider, SANGONet, has grown into a regional electronic communications network for development and human rights workers. It delivers relevant information to people working in development and aims to build capacity in organizations through the use of electronic communication. Since July 2004 SANGONet has published a monthly e-mail newsletter, Lwati ("Information" in the siSwati language), which you can subscribe to through the website.

School for International Training (SIT)

PO Box 676, Kipling Road, Brattleboro, VT 05302-0676
Tel: (802) 258-3510
Fax: (802) 258-3500
E-mail: admissions@sit.edu

SIT prepares interculturally effective leaders, professionals, and citizens committed to responsible global citizenship. SIT offers masters degrees in the fields of international education, conflict transformation, social justice in intercultural relations, sustainable development, organizational management, language teaching, and service leadership and management.

(Also listed under Alternative Travel and Study Overseas)

Transitions Abroad Publishing

PO Box 745, Bennington, VT 05201
Tel: (802) 442-4827
E-mail: info@transitionsabroad.com
Website: www.transitionsabroad.com

For 27 years Transitions Abroad has published comprehensive guides, directories, and books with practical information on alternatives to mass tourism: living, working, studying abroad, and vacationing with the people of the host country. The emphasis is on enriching, informed, affordable, and responsible travel. Visit the website or contact Transitions Abroad for more information or copies of their publications.

Volunteers for Peace, Inc. (VFP)
1034 Tiffany Road, Belmont, VT 05730
Tel: (802) 259-2759
Fax: (802) 259-2922
E-mail: vfp@vfp.org
Website: www.vfp.org

From the VFP website you can download all or part of the *VFP International Work Camp Directory*, a listing of over 2,300 opportunities for meaningful travel throughout Africa, Asia, Australia, (Western and Eastern) Europe, Latin America, and Russia. Work camps are affordable ways that North Americans of all ages can promote international goodwill through short-term community service projects in 80 countries. Two- to three-week programs cost $200 including room and board. Call, write, or e-mail VFP for a free newsletter, which includes many reports and photos from their programs.

(Also listed under International Voluntary Service Organizations)

WorkingAbroad Projects
PO Box 454, Flat 1, Brighton BN1 3ZS, East Sussex, United Kingdom
Tel/Fax: 011 (44 0) 1273-711-406
E-mail: info@workingabroad.com
Website: www.workingabroad.com

WorkingAbroad is an international networking service for volunteers and travelers. They provide personalized information service on volunteer work in over 150 countries in the following areas: administration, agriculture, community development, construction, ecotourism, education, environment, housing, human rights, journalism, medicine and nursing, organic farming, sanitation, sustainable development, teaching, wildlife surveying/management/expeditions, women's issues, and working with children. For detailed information, see the website.

(Also listed under International Voluntary Service Organizations)

Guides to International Voluntary Service

How to Live Your Dream of Volunteering Overseas. Joseph Collins, Stefano DeZerega, and Zahara Heckscher (New York: Penguin Books, 2002). Penguin USA, 375 Hudson Street, New York, NY 10014-3657, Tel: (212) 366-2000, Fax: (212) 366-2666.

The International Directory of Voluntary Work, 8th edition. Victoria Pybus (Oxford: Vacation Work Publications, 2002). Distributed in the US by The Globe Pequot Press, 246 Goose Lane, PO Box 480, Guilford, CT 06437, Main Tel: (203) 458-4500, Customer Service Tel: (888) 249-7586, Fax: (800) 820-2329, Website: *www.globepequot.com.*

International Directory of Youth Internships: With the United Nations, Its Specialized Agencies, and Non-Governmental Organizations. Michael Culligan and Cynthia T. Morehouse, eds. (New York: The Apex Press, 1994). The Apex Press, PO Box 337, Croton-on-Hudson, NY 10520, Tel/Fax: (800) 316-APEX, Website: *www.cipa-apex.org.*

The Peace Corps and More: 175 Ways to Work, Study and Travel in the Third World. Medea Benjamin and Miya Rodolfo-Sioson (San Francisco: Global Exchange, 2003). Global Exchange, 2017 Mission Street, Suite 303, San Francisco, CA 94110, Tel: (800) 497-1994 or (415) 255-7296, Website: *http://store.globalexchange.org/.*

Social Change through Voluntary Action. M. L. Dantwala, et al. (Thousand Oaks, CA: Sage Publications, Inc., 1998). Sage Publications, Inc., 2455 Teller Road, Thousand Oaks, CA 91320, Tel: (805) 499-0721, Website: *www.sagepub.com.*

Working for Global Justice Directory. (San Francisco: JustAct, 1999). JustAct, 333 Valencia Street, Suite 325, San Francisco, CA 94103, Tel: (415) 431-4204.

Guides to US Voluntary Service

Internships 2004 (Lawrenceville, NJ: Peterson's Guides, 2004). Peterson's Guides, PO Box 67005, Lawrenceville, NJ 08648, Tel: (800) 338-3282, Website: *www.petersons.com.*

A World of Options: A Guide to International Educational Exchange and Travel for Persons with Disabilities. Christa Bucks (Eugene, OR: Mobility International USA, 1997). Mobility International USA, PO Box 10767, Eugene, OR 97440, Tel: (541) 343-1284.

Publications on Travel and Tourism

Whether you intend to travel or volunteer abroad, the higher-quality tourist guides can provide background on the history, political situation, customs, and culture of countries or regions that interest you. Check the travel section of your local bookstore or contact the publishers of the series below.

Travel Publishers

Avalon Travel Publishing

1400 65th Street, Suite 250, Emeryville, CA 94608

Tel: (510) 595-3664

Fax: (510) 595-4228

Website: www.moon.com

Moon Travel Handbooks (covering the Americas, Asia, and the Pacific)

Lonely Planet Publications, Lonely Planet USA

150 Linden Street, Oakland CA 94607

Tel: (510) 893-8555

Fax: (510) 893-8563

E-mail: info@lonelyplanet.com

Website: www.lonelyplanet.com

Lonely Planet has an especially rich and detailed website, featuring bulletin boards, e-mail discussions, and up-to-the-minute information on numerous countries.

Rough Guides USA

345 Hudson Street, 4th Floor, New York, NY 10014

Tel: (212) 414-3635

Website: www.roughguides.com

Travel Guides

Alternative Travel Directory: The Complete Guide to Work, Study and Travel Overseas, seventh edition. Clayton Hubbs and David Cline, ed. (Amherst, MA: Transitions Abroad Publishing, Inc., 2002). Transitions Abroad Publishing, Inc., 18 Hulst Road, PO Box 1300, Amherst, MA 01002, Tel: (413) 256-3414, Website: *www.transitionsabroad.com.*

Fodor's Great American Learning Vacations, 1997, second edition. (New York: Fodor's Travel Publications, 1997). Random House, 1540 Broadway, New York, NY 10036.

Free Vacations and Bargain Adventures in the USA. Evelyn Kaye (Boulder, CO: Blue Panda Publications, 1998). Blue Panda Publications, 3031 Fifth Street, Boulder, CO 80304.

Rethinking Tourism, second edition. Deborah McLaren (Bloomfield, CT: Kumarian Press, 2003). Kumarian Press, 1294 Blue Hills Avenue, Bloomfield, CT 06002, Tel: (800) 289-2664 or (860) 243-2098.

Transitions Abroad. Transitions Abroad Publishing, Inc., 18 Hulst Road, PO Box 1300, Amherst, MA 01002, Tel: (413) 256-3414, Website: *www.transitionsabroad.com.* A bimonthly publication.

Volunteer Vacations: Short-Term Adventures That Will Benefit You and Others, eighth edition. Bill McMillon et al., eds. (Chicago, IL: Chicago Review Press, 2003). Chicago Review Press, 814 North Franklin, Chicago, IL 60610.

Resources for Finding Jobs in Development

Careers in International Affairs, seventh edition. School of
Foreign Service (Washington, DC: Georgetown University
Press, 2003). Georgetown University Press, 3240 Prospect
Street, NW, Washington, DC 20007, Tel: (202) 687-5889,
Website: *www.press.georgetown.edu.*

International Career Employment Weekly and *International
Employment Hotline* (monthly). International Career
Employment Center, Carlyle Corporation, 1088 Middle
River Road, Stanardsville, VA 22973, Tel: (434) 985-6444,
Fax: (434) 985-6828, E-mail: *Lisa@internationaljobs.org,*
Website: *www.internationaljobs.org.* Both publications
contain extensive overseas job listings in the public and
private sectors. Orientation is toward skilled professionals.
The center also publishes an annual guide to overseas
internships.

Work Abroad 2002, fourth edition. (Amherst, MA: Transitions
Abroad Publishing, Inc., 2002). Transitions Abroad
Publishing, Inc., 18 Hulst Road, PO Box 1300,
Amherst, MA 01002, Tel: (413) 256-3414,
Website: *www.transitionsabroad.com.*

Working for Global Justice Directory. (San Francisco: JustAct,
1999). JustAct, 333 Valencia Street, Suite 325, San Francisco,
CA 94103, Tel: (415) 431-4204.

Online Resources

Association of Voluntary Service Organizations
    Website: *www.avso.org*
    Association of national and international nonprofits based
    in Europe. Site contains volunteer opportunities, links, and
    a bulletin board.

Grass-roots.org
    Website: *www.grass-roots.org*
    Lively descriptions of over 200 grassroots organizations in
    the United States working in diverse and often innovative

ways to eliminate poverty. Robin Garr, creator of the website, has also authored a book, *Reinvesting in America,* with many more program descriptions, along with a "Getting Involved" appendix list of groups that need volunteers.

Idealist (a project of Action without Borders)

Website: *www.idealist.org*

Lists thousands of volunteer opportunities and nonprofit jobs; offers publications and resources for nonprofits and consultants.

Project Cooperating for Cooperation

Website: *www.coop4coop.org*

Comprehensive directory of development organizations and volunteer programs.

Further Reading

Chasin, Barbara H. and Richard W. Franke. *Kerala: Radical Reform as Development in an Indian State.* Oakland, CA: Food First Books, 1994.

Chinn, Erica and Kristina Taylor, eds. *The Pros and Cons of the Peace Corps.* San Francisco: JustAct.

CIVICUS. *Civil Society at the Millennium.* West Hartford, CT: Kumarian Press, 1999.

Collins, Joseph, Stefano DeZerega, and Zahara Heckscher. *How to Live Your Dream of Volunteering Overseas.* New York: Penguin Books, 2002.

Collins, Joseph, Frances Moore Lappé, and Peter Rosset with Luis Esparza. *World Hunger: Twelve Myths.* New York: Grove Press, 1998.

Etzioni, Amitai. "How Not to Squander the Volunteer Spirit," *The Christian Science Monitor,* January 27, 2003, p. 11.

Fischer, Fritz. *Making Them Like Us: Peace Corps Volunteers in the 1960s.* Washington, DC: Smithsonian Institution Press, 1998.

Kutzner, Patricia L. and Nicola Lagoudakis, with Teresa Eyring. *Who's Involved with Hunger: An Organization Guide for*

Education and Advocacy. Washington, DC: World Hunger Education Service, 1995.

Lappé, Frances Moore and Rachel Shurman. *Taking Population Seriously.* Oakland, CA: Food First Books, 1990.

MacMartin, Charley. "Peace Corps and Empire," *Covert Action Quarterly,* Winter 1991–1992, no. 39.

"One Pledge Fits All," *The San Francisco Chronicle,* November 29, 2002, p. A 28.

Razzi, Elizabeth. "What the Peace Corps Can Do For You," *Kiplinger's Personal Finance Magazine,* June 1998.

Reeves, T. Zane. *The Politics of the Peace Corps and VISTA.* Tuscaloosa, AL: University of Alabama Press, 1988.

"Russia, Citing Changing Needs, Ends Its Tie with Peace Corps," *The New York Times,* December 28, 2002, p. A4.

Schwarz, Karen. *What You Can Do for Your Country: Inside the Peace Corps—A Thirty-Year History.* New York: William Morrow, 1993.

Shahinian, Mark. "Healing Africa: Peace Corps Plan Not Enough," *Milwaukee Journal Sentinel,* September 3, 2002, p. 13A.

Zimmerman, Jonathan. "Beyond Double Consciousness: Black Peace Corps Volunteers in Africa, 1961–1971," *Journal of American History,* December 1995, vol. 82, no. 3.

Alphabetical Index

Geographical Index

MORE BOOKS FROM FOOD FIRST

Sustainable Agriculture and Development: *Transforming Food Production in Cuba*
Fernando Funes, Luis García, Martin Bourque, Nilda Pérez, and Peter Rosset

Unable to import food or farm chemicals and machines in the wake of the Soviet bloc's collapse and a tightening U.S. embargo, Cuba turned toward sustainable agriculture, organic farming, urban gardens, and other techniques to secure its food supply. This book gives details of that remarkable achievement.
Paperback, $18.95

The Future in the Balance: *Essays on Globalization and Resistance*
Walden Bello. Edited with a preface by Anuradha Mittal

A new collection of essays by third world activist and scholar Walden Bello on the myths of development as prescribed by the World Trade Organization and other institutions, and the possibility of another world based on fairness and justice.
Paperback, $13.95

Views from the South: *The Effects of Globalization and the WTO on Third World Countries*
Foreword by Jerry Mander. Afterword by Anuradha Mittal.
Edited by Sarah Anderson

This rare collection of essays by third world activists and scholars describes in pointed detail the effects of the WTO and other Bretton Woods institutions.
Paperback, $12.95

Basta! Land and the Zapatista Rebellion in Chiapas, Third Edition
George A. Collier with Elizabeth Lowery Quaratiello
Foreword by Peter Rosset

The classic on the Zapatistas in its third edition, including a preface by Roldolfo Stavenhagen.
Paperback, $16.95

America Needs Human Rights
Edited by Anuradha Mittal and Peter Rosset

This new anthology includes writings on understanding human

rights, poverty in America, and welfare reform and human rights.
Paperback, $13.95

The Paradox of Plenty: *Hunger in a Bountiful World*
Excerpts from Food First's best writings on world hunger and
what we can do to change it.
Paperback, $18.95

Education for Action: *Graduate Studies with a Focus on Social Change,*
Fourth Edition
Edited by Joan Powell
A newly updated authoritative and easy-to-use guidebook that
provides information on progressive programs in a wide variety
of fields.
Paperback, $12.95

We encourage you to buy Food First Books from your local independent bookseller: if they don't have them in stock, they can usually order
them for you fast. To find an independent bookseller in your area, go
to *www.booksense.com.*

Food First books are also available through the major online book-
sellers (Powell's, Amazon, and Barnes and Noble), and through the
Food First website, *www.foodfirst.org.* You can also order direct from
our distributor, CDS, at (800) 343-4499. If you have trouble locating a
Food First title, write, call, or e-mail us:

FOOD FIRST
398 60th Street
Oakland, CA 94618, USA
Tel: (510) 654-4400
Fax: (510) 654-4551
E-mail: foodfirst@foodfirst.org
Web: www.foodfirst.org

If you are a bookseller or other reseller, contact our distributor, CDS,
at (800) 343-4499 to order.

About Food First

FOOD FIRST, also known as the Institute for Food and Development Policy, is a nonprofit research and education-for-action center dedicated to investigating and exposing the root causes of hunger in a world of plenty. It was founded in 1975 by Frances Moore Lappé, author of the bestseller *Diet for a Small Planet,* and food policy analyst Dr. Joseph Collins. Food First research has revealed that hunger is created by concentrated economic and political power, not by scarcity. Resources and decision-making are in the hands of a wealthy few, depriving the majority of land and jobs, and therefore of food.

Hailed by *The New York Times* as "one of the most established food think tanks in the country," Food First has grown to profoundly shape the debate about hunger and development.

But Food First is more than a think tank. Through books, reports, videos, media appearances, and speaking engagements, Food First experts not only reveal the often hidden roots of hunger, they show how individuals can get involved in bringing an end to the problem. Food First inspires action by bringing to light the courageous efforts of people around the world who are creating farming and food systems that truly meet people's needs.

HOW TO BECOME A MEMBER OR INTERN OF FOOD FIRST

Become a Member of Food First

Private contributions and membership gifts form the financial base of Food First/Institute for Food and Development Policy. The success of the Institute's programs depends not only on its dedicated volunteers and staff, but on financial activists as well. Each member strengthens Food First's efforts to change a hungry world. We invite you to join Food First. As a member you will receive a 20 percent discount on all Food First books. You will also receive our quarterly publication, Food First News and Views, and timely Backgrounders that provide information and suggestions for action on current food and hunger crises in the United States and around the world. If you want to subscribe to our Internet newsletters, Food Rights Watch and We Are Fighting Back, send us an e-mail at *foodfirst@foodfirst.org*. All contributions are tax deductible.

Become an Intern for Food First

There are opportunities for interns in research, advocacy, campaigning, publishing, computers, media, and publicity at Food First. Our interns come from around the world. They are a vital part of our organization and make our work possible.

To become a member or apply to become an intern, just call, visit our website, or clip and return the attached coupon to:

FOOD FIRST
398 60th Street
Oakland, CA 94618, USA
Tel: (510) 654-4400
Fax: (510) 654-4551
E-mail: foodfirst@foodfirst.org
Web: www.foodfirst.org

You are also invited to give a gift membership to others interested in the fight to end hunger.

JOINING FOOD FIRST

❏ I want to join Food First and receive a 20% discount on this and all subsequent orders. Enclosed is my tax-deductible contribution of:

❏ $35   ❏ $50   ❏ $100   ❏ $1,000   ❏ OTHER

NAME _____

ADDRESS _____

CITY/STATE/ZIP _____

DAYTIME PHONE (_____)_____

E-MAIL _____

ORDERING FOOD FIRST MATERIALS

ITEM DESCRIPTION	QTY	UNIT COST	TOTAL

MEMBER DISCOUNT 20%	$ _____
CA RESIDENTS SALES TAX 8.75%	$ _____
SUBTOTAL	$ _____
POSTAGE 15% • UPS 20% ($2 MIN.)	$ _____
MEMBERSHIP(S)	$ _____
ADDITIONAL CONTRIBUTION	$ _____
TOTAL ENCLOSED	$ _____

PAYMENT METHOD:

❏ CHECK

❏ MONEY ORDER

❏ MASTERCARD

❏ VISA

NAME ON CARD _____

CARD NUMBER _____ EXP. DATE _____

SIGNATURE _____

MAKE CHECK OR MONEY ORDER PAYABLE TO:
FOOD FIRST • 398 60TH STREET, OAKLAND, CA 94618

For gift memberships and mailings, please see coupon on reverse side.

FOOD FIRST GIFT BOOKS

Please send a gift book to (order form on reverse side):

NAME _____

ADDRESS _____

CITY/STATE/ZIP _____

FROM _____

FOOD FIRST PUBLICATIONS CATALOGS

Please send a publications catalog to:

NAME _____

ADDRESS _____

CITY/STATE/ZIP _____

FROM _____

NAME _____

ADDRESS _____

CITY/STATE/ZIP _____

NAME _____

ADDRESS _____

CITY/STATE/ZIP _____

FOOD FIRST GIFT MEMBERSHIPS

❏ Enclosed is my tax-deductible contribution of:

❏ $35   ❏ $50   ❏ $100   ❏ $1,000   ❏ OTHER

Please send a Food First membership to:

NAME _____

ADDRESS _____

CITY/STATE/ZIP _____

FROM _____